# The Reference Shelf

# Sports in America

## Edited by Lynn M. Messina

The Reference Shelf
Volume 73 • Number 2

The H.W. Wilson Company
2001

## The Reference Shelf

The books in this series contain reprints of articles, excerpts from books, addresses on current issues, and studies of social trends in the United States and other countries. There are six separately bound numbers in each volume, all of which are usually published in the same calendar year. Numbers one through five are each devoted to a single subject, providing background information and discussion from various points of view and concluding with a subject index and comprehensive bibliography that lists books, pamphlets, and abstracts of additional articles on the subject. The final number of each volume is a collection of recent speeches, and it contains a cumulative speaker index. Books in the series may be purchased individually or on subscription.

Library of Congress has cataloged this serial title as follows:

Sports in America/ edited by Lynn M. Messina.
p. cm.— (The reference shelf ; v. 73, no. 2)
Includes bibliographical references and index.
ISBN 0-8242-0999-0 (pbk)
1. Sports—United States. I. Messina, Lynn M. II. Series.

GV583 .S6852 2001
796'.0973—dc21 00-054995



Visit H.W. Wilson's Web site: www.hwwilson.com

Printed in the United States of America

# Contents

# *Preface*

T. S. Eliot may have called April the "cruelest month," but for American sports fans and athletes, the fun is just beginning. No sooner have fans recovered from their Superbowl revelry and March Madness when baseball's Opening Day arrives, the Master's golf tournament begins, the NFL holds its annual college draft, and professional basketball and hockey anticipate the nearly two-month-long playoffs before crowning their champions. Across the country, snows are melting, enabling people to resume biking, roller blading, skate boarding, and organizing little league teams and youth soccer matches. In America, playing sports is about exploring and exploiting freedom while challenging expectations. The controlled conflict that takes place on the field or in the arena gives athletes the chance to shine and spectators the chance to dream—about running faster, throwing harder, scoring higher, or hitting a ball farther than anyone else. The fans marvel at their favorite athletes, who push and sometimes smash the boundaries and standards set for them, as when Barry Bonds smacks a home run out of Pacific Bell Park that splashes into McCovey Cove, or Marion Jones sprints through yet another world record.

This volume, while not intended to be comprehensive, is meant to explore various aspects of the games, athletes, scandals, and concerns that color the worlds of American amateur and professional sports today. The articles chosen survey the topic of sports in America from several perspectives—those of the athletes, the fans, the businessmen, and the media. The writers consider the appeal of certain sports, the athletes who inspire and those who disappoint, and the billion-dollar industry that has developed to showcase the talents of a few gifted individuals.

The book is divided into six sections, each addressing American sports from a different angle. The articles in Section I, "America's Pastimes," consider the singular appeal of some of the most popular sports, including football, baseball, golf, NASCAR, and tennis, as well as women athletes. Section II, "Youth Sports," looks at several important issues concerning child and teenage athletes, such as the importance of prioritizing fun over accomplishment, participation by disabled children, the growing pressures on children participating in sports, the rising violence among parents at their children's games, and the dangers to children who suffer repeat injuries. Section III, "College and Semipro Sports," examines organizational attempts to achieve gender and financial equity for college athletes, the balancing of academics and athletic participation, the role of race in college sports, plans for basketball's new minor league, and the economic and social advantages of minor league baseball.

The second half of the book looks primarily at professional sports, beginning with Section IV, "The Good, the Great, and the Ugly," which focuses on the character and personality of professional athletes. These individuals include some of the 20th century's greatest players, such as Tiger Woods, Michael Jordan, Wayne Gretzkey, and John Elway; those who inspire others with their performances, such as Lance Armstrong; and those whose off-the-field behavior brings shame to themselves and their sports. The final article in the section considers the need to reform boxing in order to improve the quality of matches and showcase the sport's best athletes. The articles in Section V, "The Business of Sports," then look at the big business of sports, considering the history of the professional sports industry in America; the manner in and degree to which owners profit from their teams; the effect of high ticket prices on attendance; the notion of extending the influence of major league franchises abroad; and the marketing of extreme sports to young people. The book's final section, "The Olympics," looks at those games, beginning with the Special Olympics, then moving on to one athlete's perspective on the true meaning of the Olympic Games, and the bribery and drug scandals that have recently tarnished the Olympic image.

I would like to thank the authors and publications that gave permission for their work to be reprinted in this volume. I would also like to thank Jacqueline Latif, Norris Smith, Sandra Watson, Sara Yoo, and the staff of the General Reference division for their patience and assistance in the production of this book.

**Lynn M. Messina**
**April 2001**

# I. America's Pastimes

John Froshauer/AP

# *Editor's Introduction*

The appeal of sports is complicated, varying as much from individual to individual as from sport to sport. Americans take their sports spectatorship and participation very seriously, deriving a variety of pleasures and benefits from their experiences. While fans savor the vicarious thrill of watching their favorite athletes and teams excel, the participants themselves learn what ABC's *Wide World of Sports* called "the thrill of victory and the agony of defeat." The articles chosen for Section I, which consider some of the most popular sports in America today, explore these issues by attempting to answer several important questions: Can participation in sports genuinely enrich our lives? What gives a sport its appeal? What criteria should we apply when assessing whether or not a sport is actually a sport? Which athletes are more exciting to watch—men or women? How much competitive aggression is too much?

The first article in this section is "Sports and Life: Lessons to Be Learned" by former NFL quarterback Jeff Kemp. As Kemp reflects upon his amateur and professional careers, he describes six specific areas in which an athlete may grow from playing organized sports: humility, honesty, value systems, leadership, perseverance, and spirit. In the next article, "Hitting the Sweet Spot," Stephen Lehman describes the joys of another sport—baseball—from a spectator's perspective, considering the significance of that sport in American society. Jay Stuller then looks at golf to determine if it is, indeed, a sport, in "Out of Their League." NASCAR, arguably the nation's most popular spectator sport, is the subject of the article "An American Sport Revs Up," which describes the moral and political attitudes of drivers such as Jeff Gordon and Junior Johnson, and their fans.

The increasing popularity of female athletes and women's sports has been one of the most interesting stories of the last decade. Not only have such organizations as the WNBA, the U.S. Women's World Cup soccer team, and superstars like the sisters Venus and Serena Williams given young girls role models in the field of athletic competition, but many assert that their style of play is more exciting than that of their male counterparts. Sara Hammel and Anna Mulrine consider this phenomenon in "They Got More Than Just Game," where they look at the growing appeal of women's sports for spectators of both genders. By focusing specifically on women's tennis, Patrick Hruby, in "Tennis Racket," considers the growing celebrity status of female players, along with the increase in endorsement revenue that has accompanied it.

# Sports and Life: Lessons to Be Learned[1]

BY JEFF KEMP
*USA TODAY*, MARCH 1999

We live in an age when, too often, rules are scorned; values are turned upside down; principles are replaced by expediency; and character has been sacrificed for popularity. Individual athletes sometimes are the worst offenders, but not as often as one might think. That is because sports teach important moral lessons athletes can apply on and off the playing field.

Many people dream of being a professional athlete. For me, the dream seemed to be within reach because my father, Jack Kemp, an outstanding quarterback, played for the American Football League's Buffalo Bills (prior to the AFL's 1970 merger with the National Football League). The trouble was, I was not very good! I was a third-string football player through most of junior high and high school and for two years at Dartmouth College. I was not anyone's idea of a "hot prospect." After graduation, I was passed over by NFL scouts. When I finally was asked to join the Los Angeles Rams in 1981 as a free agent, I was designated as fifth-string quarterback.

## Humility

It was a 50-to-1 shot that I would survive training camp. Rookies were the only players required to show up for the first week of camp. There were dozens competing for the few spots open on the team.

After two days, a young boy approached me as I was walking off the field. He asked if he could carry my helmet to the locker room. It was a long way, but I said, "Sure, I think you can handle that." The next morning, he showed up before practice and offered to carry my helmet and shoulder pads, and he was there again after practice offering the same service. So it went for the rest of the week.

On the last day, as we were departing the field, my young assistant said, "Jeff, can I ask you a question?" (We were on a first-name basis by then.) I thought, "This is my first fan! He is going to

---

1. Article by Jeff Kemp from *USA Today* March 1999. 

ask me for an autograph." He then inquired, "When do the good football players come to camp?" Right then and there, I learned a lesson in humility from a seven-year-old boy.

In my first three NFL seasons, I was forced to learn the same lesson over and over again. During that time, I threw just 31 passes. Nevertheless, by 1984, I had managed to outlast the five NFL quarterbacks who had been ahead of me. With the Rams' record standing at 1-2, I took over for injured quarterback Vince Ferragamo and earned my first start against the Cincinnati Bengals, eventually leading the Rams to nine more victories and a playoff berth.

The next season, I returned to the bench as a backup quarterback. Humility, I was compelled to remind myself, was a good thing. It helped me appreciate what I had and avoid dwelling on what I did not have. It prevented complaining, which drains the spirit and unity of any group. It also led me to persevere and be ready whenever opportunity presented itself.

In 1986, I was traded to the San Francisco 49ers as a backup for Joe Montana. While he was sidelined with a back injury, I was called upon to take over the offense. We won against the New Orleans Saints, Miami Dolphins, and Indianapolis Colts, primarily because wide receiver Jerry Rice reached the end zone with a number of my touchdown passes. As soon as Montana recovered, however, I was again relegated to the bench. At about the same time, I received a fan letter that read:

> Dear Jeff,
>
> As Joe Montana returns, you'll probably feel like you were shoveled off to the side. Well, just remember, Joe Montana is the greatest quarterback to ever play the game. You should feel lucky to have even played on his team.

The author of the letter sang Montana's praises for another full paragraph and then closed with a real zinger: "P.S. You are not as bad as some people might say." With fans like this, I never had to worry that my head would grow too big for my helmet.

Honesty

The importance of honesty colors all the rest of life. Why is truth so important? It is because respect, relationships, and unity all depend on truth. If you can not be honest with people, you can not have healthy relationships. A family can't stick together without honesty and neither can a nation—or, for that matter, an athletic team.

Sports taught me about the vital importance of honesty. They forced me to ask questions: Am I committed to the truth? Am I willing to let my flaws be revealed so that I can do something about them? In particular, football showed me that talk is cheap. We could boast that we were going to do this or that, but it wasn't until we actually were out on the playing field that the truth was revealed. We completed passes or we did not. We made it to the end zone or we fell short. We won or we lost. There was plenty of game film footage to provide an objective appraisal of our strengths and weaknesses.

I learned that if you try to hide from the truth, you never will grow. Without truth, I couldn't trust my teammates and they couldn't trust me. To have a championship season, follow a well-traveled course, and live a significant and happy life, we need a fixed point of reference. We must seek and face the truth. None of us lives up to the perfect standard of always being true and always being honest, but we need to aim at this goal if our lives, families, businesses, and communities are to prosper.

In this context, sports taught me that there are rules of life I must heed. What would a football field be like if there were no sidelines, end zones, or yard markers? What if the goal posts were moved in the middle of a game? What would basketball be like if the court had no boundaries and the player dribbling the ball had no limitations? What would keep him from running into the bleacher section? Who would say he needed to make a basket to score? What would a track meet be like? Who would determine the winners in a race if the officials threw away their stopwatches and turned their backs on the runners? Without life's rules—that is, without universally acknowledged truths—there is no form, no function, no way to prefer one kind of action or outcome over another.

***Sports are elevated life. They are noble and ignoble, beautiful and ugly.***

**Value Systems**

Sports are elevated life. They are noble and ignoble, beautiful and ugly. They reveal the best and worst of human nature in an action-packed arena dominated by intense emotion. When sports commentators repeat the old cliché about "the thrill of victory and the agony of defeat," we all know exactly what they are talking about. As players or spectators, we have experienced both. Yet, underneath the adrenaline rush is something even more powerful: our value system.

Sports, in other words, reveal what we treasure most. In 1988, I was playing for the Seattle Seahawks against my old team, the 49ers, when I learned firsthand that there are two competing value systems. I wasn't bitter that my old team had traded me, but I wanted to beat them all the same. Quarterback Dave Krieg had been injured, and I was to start. I had a great week of practice and felt totally prepared. I entered the Kingdom in Seattle brimming with excitement. I envisioned leading my team to victory and establishing myself as the Seahawks' starter.

Coming out of the pregame meal, one of the offensive coaches put his arm around me and strongly affirmed his faith in me: "I want you to know how happy I am that you are the Seahawk quarterback. I've been waiting for this day." I felt honored, valued, esteemed. This was going to be a great day!

Well, we ran the ball on our first two plays, and we didn't gain much. On third down and eight, I threw to Hall of Famer wide receiver Steve Largent, who split two defenders. The pass hit him right in the hands, yet he dropped the ball. Next to Jerry Rice, Largent is, statistically speaking, the greatest receiver in history. He also is one of my best friends. All I could do at that moment was chuckle and moan, "Steve, what's the matter? You never drop the ball. Why are you doing this to me?"

After that, he didn't make any mistakes, but I did. In fact, I played the worst game of my life. At the end of the first half, the 49ers were ahead 28-0. Every person in the Kingdome, with the exception of my wife (and there isn't even a witness to vouch for her), was booing me. Have you ever heard nearly 60,000 people booing you? It's quite an experience.

As I came off the field at halftime, I knew that I might be benched, but I wasn't defeated. Ever since I had been a small boy, my father had been drumming into my head British Prime Minister Winston Churchill's brave words to the students at Harrow School in the dark days of 1941: "Never give in, never give in, never, never, never, never—in nothing, great or small, large or petty—never give in except to convictions of honor and good sense."

I waded through the players to find the coach who had been so supportive before the game. I wanted to discuss some offensive strategies that might turn things around in the second half. As I approached him and began, "Coach . . .," he turned his back on me without a word. Then he called to another quarterback, put his arm around him, and began to discuss plays that player would run in the second half.

Now, I understood that I was being taken out of the game. That made sense. I was hoping it wouldn't happen, but I understood. However, that coach didn't say one word to me for the rest of the game, even though we stood next to each other on the sidelines. Nor did he say anything on Monday when we watched the game films. For about a month, there was complete rejection. He simply couldn't deal with the fact that I hadn't lived up to his hopes, that I hadn't helped the team succeed. He rejected me relationally because my performance fell short.

I discovered during this painful episode a faulty value system that is conditional and performance-based. It rejects relationships and dishonors the diverse yet equal value of every person. My coach, as well as other coaches and even owners, not only was exerting, but feeling the pressure of this value system, which has been adopted by so many in business and the culture at large.

My career slowly, steadily had been rising, and now, all of a sud-

---

***Performance and competition are important, as are rewards and incentives, but none of these things enhances or demeans the value of an individual.***

---

den, it seemed it was on a speedy downward course. The fifth-stringer had made it to first string only to be benched, booed by the crowd, and shunned by his own coach. It looked like my last chance to succeed had come and gone.

Eventually, though, I found renewed hope and confidence—through a transcendent value system, which is quite different. It is an unconditional, relational, and character-based value system. It leads us to treat others as we wish to be treated. Of course, performance and competition are important, as are rewards and incentives, but none of these things enhances or demeans the value of an individual.

From then on, I began to appreciate another important moral lesson sports taught me: My relationship with a person should not be based on how well I like his "external packaging." What does he look like? What has she accomplished? How much money does he have? How successful is he? How popular is she? How many touchdowns has he thrown? These conditional valuations are corrosive. They make kids so insecure that they are afraid to make friends. They make adults so insecure that they make moral compromises, often sacrificing marriage, family, faith, and ethics on the altar of success. It is a vain effort, however, for there is no true success apart from these things.

This lesson was underscored by my experience at the Special Olympics, where I loved the vital role of "huggers." As runners cross the finish line in track events, there are huggers waiting for each and every one of them. A hugger's only job is to embrace the runners with love and tell them, "Terrific job! You looked great out there."

Winning is important. I never would disparage it. Still, doesn't it feel good to have someone to hug you, whether you have won or lost—to value you for your relationship, not just your performance?

**Leadership**

Sports, and quarterbacking in particular, provide invaluable lessons in leadership that are applicable to everyone, in all situations. A leader is not defined solely by his or her position. Everyone is a leader. Even backup quarterbacks. In life, most of us will spend a fair amount of time on the bench, but that doesn't mean we aren't in the game. We constantly are influencing and shaping the lives of countless people.

***We don't have to be first-stringers to have an impact.***

We don't have to be first-stringers to have an impact. I wasn't Joe Montana. I wasn't Denver Broncos quarterback John Elway, either. Nonetheless, there were things I could do to help my team and teammates. I could be a role model of preparation and commitment, inspiring others to their best effort. When a young player confided that he had marital problems, I could share what I learned from the Bible about commitment and spiritual comfort in times of trouble. When a rookie was scared to death that he was going to get cut, I could give him encouragement: "Hey, I saw how well you ran today. You have a good chance!" As my wife Stacy pointed out, focusing on encouraging others also kept my mind off the stress of surviving each summer's roster cuts.

For instance, there was the punter who once fouled up so badly that our team lost two yards. The coaches were screaming epithets at him. I said to myself, "This is the only punter we've got! He may have to go back into the game, and I want him to do well." I walked up to him and said, "It's okay, man. You'll get it right next time." I spoke too loudly, and one of the coaches started hollering at me. Still, some of the heat had been deflected from the punter.

Gary Kubiak, the quarterback coach for the Broncos, was the backup to Elway for many years. Kubiak rarely got to play, but today he is one of the smartest and most respected assistant coaches in the business. That's because he has a leadership mentality. He has said, "Everyone has an influence on some other person. You must always assume that your actions will influence another." No wonder Kubiak helped the Broncos become 1998 and 1999 Super Bowl champions. Every person's leadership counts, and the best leaders model, serve, and inspire.

Vision, not sight, is what makes people truly see. The deaf and blind lecturer Helen Keller once was asked, "Is there anything worse than not having your sight?" She responded earnestly, "Oh yes, it would be much worse to have your sight, but not to have vision." Think of all the opportunities and responsibilities that are lost today because we are so busy looking at what is two feet in front of us.

Vision has allowed me to throw footballs when I could not see the receiver. Playing for the Philadelphia Eagles, I threw one to tight end Keith Jackson just before a blitzing pass rusher knocked me off my feet. I couldn't see Jackson and he couldn't see me, but we each knew what to do. We had visualized what our responses would be in that kind of situation many times before. Jackson was right where I envisioned. He caught my blind pass and ran for a touchdown.

I learned to see not only where I was, but where I wanted to be in the future. The best players—in life as well as in football—never are content to win one game. They want to win the next game, too, and the one after that. This requires long-term planning and commitment.

Vision also is about seeing opportunity when it seems least likely. My parents reinforced this lesson. For example, when my college football team lost a game and I didn't even get to play, my father consoled me by saying, "You looked great today." Stunned, I replied, "What?" He insisted, "Yes, you looked great. I saw you warming up. The ball was really spinning. Your day is going to come, Jeff. You'll get your chance. Think like a starter." His optimism left no room for my shortsighted pessimism.

Vision is what has led me and my teammates to make sacrifices gladly. When I was playing for the 49ers, Coach Bill Walsh took special care to explain a certain play-action pass to the entire offense. More than one player grumbled, "Why do I need to learn what the other guys are doing?," but Walsh knew exactly what he was doing. He was giving a vision of a play that would demand a great deal of us. We were to fool our opponents into thinking it was a run.

Walsh warned the linemen that they would have to fall forward, right into their opponents' knees. If they were lucky, they would only suffer swollen, bloody hands from the cleats of their opponents' shoes. He told the halfback that he would have to dive over the line of scrimmage, holding his hands to his stomach and leaving his head completely unprotected, in order to make the other team believe that he had the ball. He told me that after I faked the handoff, lured the free safety two steps forward, turned, and passed the ball to Jerry Rice, I would end up flat on my back when the 260-pound unblocked defensive end hit me, after realizing it was a pass.

That's exactly what did happen—five times in six weeks. We scored a touchdown on every derivation of that play during the 1986 season. For most of the players involved, this play did not add one yard to their stat sheets, but that didn't matter. The vision Walsh provided led them to trust one another and to make sacrifices.

**Perseverance**

Vision has helped me develop appreciation for the value of perseverance in the face of adversity. For 19 of my 20 years in amateur and professional football, I was not the starting quarterback going into training camp. As a pro, I was a fifth-stringer, a fourth-stringer, a third-stringer, a second-stringer, and a first-stringer, but it was not always a matter of forward motion. Sometimes, I was set back, traded, or cut. I persevered, however, trusting my vision, rather than my sight.

My last game as a professional football player was the season finale against the Washington Redskins in December, 1991. The Redskins (who would go on to win the Super Bowl in January) had lost just one game all season. My team, the Eagles, trailed 19-7 in the final quarter. The Redskins were stopping our runs, batting down my passes, and beating me up. I had been sacked twice and knocked down at least half a dozen times. At one point when I came off the field, the offensive linemen apologized to me for the lack of protection. The offensive line coach, stymied and demoralized, also apologized. I responded, "This is ridiculous! Let's get down to work and play to win. We aren't going to lose."

Sure, it looked as though I couldn't get anything done that day. My opponents were killing me before I could even throw the ball. Nevertheless, I felt in the game. I was sharp and confident. I figured that we might be able to turn things around if the Redskins made even one error.

Eventually, they did. Enjoying a huge lead, they started playing not to lose instead of playing to win. We completed two touchdown passes and kicked a field goal at the end of the game that beat them. That season's closing victory was a testimony to perseverance.

**Spirit**

In sports and life, we need long-term vision or we never will reach our goals. We must be persistent, which means remaining steadfast in purpose. Honesty and an unconditional value system shape the noblest of purposes. We need to remember how important relationships, family, and God's unconditional love are. I know that these things gave me the peace to play a game that has an incredible amount of pressure and insecurity, where I had to earn my spot every game and get my job back every year. I know that they are what will help our culture recover its vision of what is important and what is worth defending—family, marriage, responsibility, trust, and truth.

Sports teach positive lessons that enrich America even while revealing its flaws. Sports remind us that we are all leaders and we influence the lives of others. In the final analysis, though, it is our spirit that determines what we draw out of sports and what we draw out of life.

# Hitting the Sweet Spot[2]

BY STEPHEN LEHMAN
*ELYSIAN FIELDS QUARTERLY,* SUMMER 1998

I had never been to Dallas, and I felt certain I could live a perfectly happy and fulfilled life without ever getting Lone Star dust on my very plain, well-worn Tony Lamas. To my mind, just about the only decent things besides those boots ever to come out of Texas were Willie Nelson and Molly Ivins. But when the opportunity arose to attend a conference in Big D last May as part of my real job (you didn't think being editor of a baseball journal paid the rent, did you?), I jumped at it, for two reasons: first, I'd never been to the Ballpark at Arlington; second, Talmage Boston lives in Dallas.

Unless you live in Dallas or are a diligent, long-time reader of *EFQ*, you may not have heard of Talmage. A successful civil attorney, Talmage is a baseball fanatic—not merely a fan, not just someone who loves the game, but a full-fledged, card-carrying, baseball-fevered lunatic—who, in addition to penning several articles for *EFQ* a few years back, authored *1939: Baseball's Pivotal Year* (Summit, 1995), one chapter of which (on Bill McKechnie) was excerpted in this journal. When I called Talmage to see if we could meet to catch a ball game together, his first concern was how to arrange tickets (and rearrange his busy schedule) so we could see all four Rangers games. I assured him one game would be sufficient—I was there to work, after all—but that was my first tip-off that Texas hospitality is more than just Chamber of Commerce hype.

I arrived on a Wednesday, called Talmage, and set a date to meet for lunch the next day, with a trip to Arlington for a Rangers-Mariners tilt later Thursday evening. That first night, though, I listened to the local game on the radio while watching the Braves and Rockies on TBS (with the mute button on). The Rangers, already winners of three straight, came from six runs down against the notoriously inept Seattle bullpen to win 8 to 7 in their last at bat.

I met Talmage the next day at his law firm, a sprawling enterprise that took up several floors of the Renaissance Tower and employed some 240 attorneys—this was Texas, after all—and he immediately whisked me to his office, which was, by any standards, fairly packed with baseball paintings, mementos, and memorabilia. Talmage was even more gregarious and welcoming in person, something I'd not

2. Article by Stephen Lehman from *Elysian Fields Quarterly* Summer 1998. 

have thought possible, and he immediately launched into baseball stories: who he'd gotten to meet, interview, talk to, get autographs from. But this was neither bravado nor one-upmanship. This was joy—the pure baseball joy of a little kid who'd had the indescribably good luck of having a major league foul ball come his way a week after breaking in his new fielder's glove.

Trading baseball stories as quickly as we could get the words out, we drove out to The Ballpark at Arlington for lunch at The Front Row (a TGI Friday's restaurant) in a booth overlooking the field from above the right-center field upper deck, followed by a whirl-

***Loving baseball . . . is one of the most powerful connecting forces I know of. It crosses all manner of divides: class, race, culture, and ideology.***

wind tour of the Legends of the Game Baseball Museum and Learning Center, a combination Hall of Fame slice and delightful interactive children's exhibit, and the Rangers front office. Then back to downtown Dallas.

I write all this not because it is should be of particular interest to anyone other than me, but to make a point: baseball, or rather, loving baseball, is one of the most powerful connecting forces I know of. It crosses all manner of divides: class, race, culture, and ideology. Loving the game, and possessing that measure of knowledge about it which comes to those who love it well over time, cuts through all that crap. Or at least it suspends it, keeps it at bay for a period of time—say nine innings or so of time, long enough to be human with one another.

I don't mean to belittle the pressing issues of our day, or suggest that baseball is some kind of civic paragon or cultural palliative. We all know that the game often reflects all the pain and conflict and political squabbling of the society. Nor do I endorse using baseball as some kind of drug, some kind of mind-numbing, escapist strategy. On the contrary, as long-time readers of this journal can attest, I believe baseball can and should be used, at times, to clarify in the microcosm the dysfunctions and systemic failures of the macrocosm. But the Pastime has a more significant role to play in society, I believe, than merely mirroring our cultural defects, and that role is modeling potential solutions. And that's what I want to talk about here, because I think the solutions ultimately always have to do with forging common ground, with finding common values from which to grow a larger social dialogue, with seeing each other not first as Democrats or Republicans, capitalists or socialists, or by ethnic, gender, or sexual orientation labels, but as human beings trying to live with integrity and compassion in the physical world. And one way to start along that path is to be in a place of worship and joy where we see each other first as simply baseball fans.

The game that night at Arlington embodied both the sensual joys of baseball and the human connections it can offer. I sat next to Talmage's friend Paul Rogers, former dean of the SMU law school and co-author, with Hall of Fame pitcher Robin Roberts, of *The Whiz Kids and the 1950 Pennant* (Temple University Press, 1996). Paul and I hit it off right away and, as had happened with Talmage, we started in immediately trading baseball stories. Meanwhile, a strange and beautiful game unfolded before us: Griffey hit a 425 foot home run in the one spot where a ball could actually leave the park, though this particular dinger came up short, and finished the game just a single shy of completing the cycle; the Rangers came from 5 runs back to win yet again in their last at bat, 9 to 8 this time (again, not all that surprising since it was at the expense of Seattle's relief corps, notably the hapless Bobby Ayala). It was a gorgeous night, warm but not hot, neither dry nor humid. Above all, it was *outdoors*. In the ninth, a fan jumped the railing to help Johnny Oates argue a close call with the third base ump Brian O'Nora (I'd never seen *that* before), and Juan Gonzalez continued his awesome RBI barrage that has him on track to shatter Hack Wilson's impossible 190 singleseason mark. (I know, won't happen. But it's still amazing to see a guy hit like that, night after night, with runners in scoring position.)

Paul proposed the story-telling category of "stupidest things ever to happen in baseball," and began with a tale he'd heard from Robin Roberts (and recounted in their book): In the first game of a doubleheader against the Cubs at Wrigley Field, teammates Johnny Blatnick, Del Ennis, and Dick Sisler spotted Roberts a 2-0 lead. The Cubs came back in the sixth to tie it on hits by Eddie Waitkus, Phil Cavaretta, and Andy Pafko, and it stayed that way until the bottom of the ninth when Roberts surrendered a one-out single to Cub pitcher Johnny Schmitz. A force play followed, but so did another single, to Waitkus again, and Roberts' control deserted him. He hit Cavaretta in the gut to load them up, and then, on the very next pitch, repeated the feat, this time at the expense of Pafko's rib cage. As Roberts started toward the dugout, dejected over blowing the game, Pafko decided to take offense at his free pass and began to charge the mound. First base coach Hard Rock Johnson headed him off however, grabbing his shirt and yelling, "You dumb SOB, he wasn't throwing at you, he just lost the game!"

I countered with something I'd seen in Syracuse in 1984, in a AAA game between the Chiefs and the Rochester Red Wings. Bottom of the ninth, tie score, runners on first and third, one out. The Chiefs' batter smashed a scorching line drive down the left field line which started in fair territory but was obviously hooking foul. The Rochester left fielder, clearly the most fleet-footed of outfield patrolmen, took off like the proverbial bat out of hell and made a diving, back-hand, miraculous catch of the ball about eight feet outside the foul line. The winning run, of course, moseyed home. The left fielder, still apparently unaware of the circumstance, came trotting triumphantly homeward only to see his red-faced skipper, steam rising from his collar like the spout of a screaming tea kettle, emerge from the dugout and plant himself somewhere north of the coaching box, hands on hips, facing his errant charge. The fielder slowed his gait and stopped, the dawn breaking suddenly through the dark night of his befuddled senses, and his head slowly tipped forward until his chin came to rest against the top button of his uniform shirt. There was not a person in the ballpark, not even the most idealistic, baseball-crazed little kid, who would have wanted to stand in that ballplayer's spikes at that moment. Oh, the humanity.

Ten days later and I'm in Wrigley Field on consecutive nights with long-time friend and ballpark architecture maven Philip Bess, author of *City Baseball Magic: Plain Talk and Uncommon Sense about Cities and Baseball Parks.* (We were joined the second night by Save Our Sox activist Mary O'Connell and *EFQ* contributor Betty Christiansen.) As in Texas, the home team won while I was there (I've seen the locals lose only in Minnesota so far this year), concluding a sweep of the feared Braves and beginning a two-game thrashing of the pathetic, decimated World Champion Marlins. (The Cubs next swept the cross-town rival White Sox, and their streak stands at nine games as of this writing.) Now I'm a Cardinals fan, and by all accounts I should have been cheering on the visitors in order to bring the Chicago Nationals back to the pack. Yet sitting in Phil's third base line upper deck seats—which, by the way, seemed to be every bit as close to the playing field as the $25 seat I'd occupied in Arlington, yet in the Friendly Confines it cost only nine bucks—I couldn't help but cheer along with the home crowd. The whole experience was simply too intoxicating to spoil by maintaining proper allegiances.

While The Ballpark at Arlington is very pretty, with some truly outstanding features, such as the molded relief metopes of Texas and baseball history adorning the facade, it seems a bit of a mishmash of styles and design; it's not completely clear what the architects had in mind other than to include as many desirable features as possible (desired by just about anybody—the park seems an effort to offer all things to all people). My main objection to Arlington, however, would probably apply to any of the new parks: it's primary focus seems to be to maximize the ways in which the patrons of the game can be separated from their cash. Because it's a suburban site, parking is plentiful and free (I think), but beyond that, The Ballpark is a hive of consumerist activity, a la the so-called New Comiskey. I suspect the same is true of Coors and Camden Yards and the Jake, though I've not had the pleasure as yet to visit those venues.

Wrigley is decidedly different. To borrow Phil's phrase, it's still reasonably civilized. You can sit closer to the game for less money, and you can bring your own food into the park as long as it's not in a can or a bottle. There's no rock and roll blaring at you between innings, no commercials that aren't on billboards on the buildings across the streets. These seemingly minor aspects contribute to

***Despite the myriad problems it faces, baseball in its best contexts is still . . . beautiful, sophisticated, sensual, daring, communal.***

what is the biggest difference, however, between where the Cubs play and almost any other ball field: Wrigley is accessible to its community. In fact, it *anchors* its community: it's located in a city block in a residential urban neighborhood; it's right off the El and numerous bus routes, providing public transportation access to anyone in the city. (God forbid you should want to attend a Rangers game but don't have a car—there are probably shuttles from somewhere to there, but I never caught wind of them.) As in Arlington, it's a friendly environment, but unlike The Ballpark, it's confined, primarily by the neighborhood from which it arises—hence it's nickname. That trait creates a particular social intimacy that is the embodiment of what I was trying to get at earlier in this piece: baseball as interpersonal and social connective tissue. In a divided and divisive world, something that brings people together to enjoy a beautiful, complex, endlessly interesting contest of wits, physical prowess, and shifting strategies is welcome and much-needed. If it ties them to neighborhood (and city and then metropolitan area, and so on), as Wrigley does, so much the better. For despite the myriad problems it faces, baseball in its best contexts is still all those great things: beautiful, sophisticated, sensual, daring, communal.

I haven't seen my beloved (and mightily struggling) Cardinals yet this year, and I'll miss the chance to catch them at the Metrodome. The only good I can see to come out of interleague play would be the opportunity to see my team in the flesh, even if it happened in that huge blister of a stadium we have in Minnesota. (It's probably just as well that I'll be out of town. The last time I saw the Cards at the Dome was to watch them get pulverized in Game Two of the 1987 World Series. I was the guy with the red ball cap and sour face who stayed in his seat in the left field bleachers for the entire game.) But as consolation, it's on to San Francisco for the SABR convention, where I'll renew old baseball acquaintances and make new ones, and enjoy my first ever visit to Candlestick Park (not 3Com or 4Com or any other Com, as far as I'm concerned). I may live in Minnesota, but I still plan to take a jacket. After that, I'll visit the fountains of Kansas City's Kaufman Stadium (I'll accept that change—at least it's named for a human being) with my father, with a trip to the Negro Leagues Baseball Museum there on the side.

All in all, a pretty darn good baseball summer. But I have to tell you: it wouldn't be half as fun without Talmage and Paul and Phil and Mary and my father. For me, the greatest baseball joy of all is the opportunity to share the pleasures of the game with somebody—or somebodies—else.

# Out of Their League[3]

BY JAY STULLER
*SENIOR GOLFER,* JULY 2000

Sitting in a grandstand at the Silverado Country Club in Napa, California, last fall, Larry Laoretti flicked an ash from his cigar and mused about one difference between his current profession and his favorite childhood sports. "I guess what's most frustrating," he allows, "is that you can't play defense in golf."

Laoretti's lament is derived from his experience as a baseball, basketball and football star at Mahopac High School on Long Island. "You know, I've often thought about if I ever get in the hunt again. Say the guy I'm paired with has a three-footer on the final hole to tie or take the tournament away from me. Wouldn't it be great if I could go up and just pop him like a blitzing safety hits a quarterback?"

Laoretti would get away without a flag or a 15-yard penalty. Of course, he'd get DQ-ed and probably banned from the Senior PGA Tour. Within the genteel realm of golf, busting an opponent with a forearm shiver would generate more outrage than Mike Tyson's snacking on Evander Holyfield's ear.

That lack of fast-motion contact and dearth of physical aggression are why many critics argue that golf is not a sport. The game's defenders are told that it's less athlectically demanding since there are no stampeding Reggie Whites; no malevolent Randy Johnsons hurling Titleists under your chin. The primary task is to hit a stationary sphere, they argue, which renders the game comparable to Little League T-ball. Such comparisons have dogged the game for years, but as athletes from other sports obsess about their own battles with the dimpled white ball, it's worth noting that many golfers, especially on the senior tour, may be able to draw from their own athletic experiences. "When our generation came of age, golf wasn't viewed as much of a sport, at least compared to other 10 competitive games," says Gary McCord, who played basketball for Jerry Tarkanian at Riverside City College—now the University of California at Riverside. "When I was in high school you were a geek if you played golf. I proudly had my baseball and basketball letters on the front of my letterman's jacket. But this is the truth: I actually sewed my golf letter onto the inside of the jacket."

---

3. Article by Jay Stuller from *Senior Golfer* July 2000. Copyright © Times Mirror Magazines.

It's still fairly common to hear disparaging remarks about golf's athletic demands. Most of us shrug it off, but tour pros are surprisingly sensitive to the topic.

"Oh no, not the 'golfers-aren't-real-athletes thing,'" says Graham Marsh, his body stiffening as he recoils from the discussion. The ever-gracious Swampy strains to remain polite, but "No. No. No," is all he can muster.

Marsh is swiftly assured that this discussion may correct a misperception, but the subject, even presented in jest, hits a nerve. It's clear that the Australian star, who had a future as a first-class cricket player until he broke his arm as a youngster, has thoughtfully navigated this line of logic at least a few times before.

"It really must start with how you describe athletic performance" Marsh explains. "The idea of athletics, at least as we know them, goes back to the Greek Olympics. Much of that involved running or lifting heavy weights. So, are the only measures of athleticism brute strength or a high aerobic capacity?"

***"Are the only measures of athleticism brute strength or a high aerobic capacity?"*— Graham Marsh, Australian cricket player.**

As various sports developed, Marsh adds, "different kinds of skills were required. Eye-hand coordination, a fine sense of balance, reaction times, a need to perform under pressure. Then some sports required those fine skills and strength and high aerobic capacity. But each activity is different. Compare an NFL linebacker who plays only half the game and never touches the ball, and an Australian Rules player who runs for 100 minutes, dives for the ball with both hands and kicks it. Is one an athlete and the other not?"

They're both athletes, of course, and so are professional golfers. In fact, at its highest level the game requires a demanding set of athletic skills that aren't always obvious to the casual observer. That became apparent to me nearly 20 years ago when I was commissioned by *Playboy* magazine to determine "The Toughest Job in Sports." Several leading sports scientists and sports psychologists helped me develop 20 separate ratings categories of things demanded in sport. These included the need for physical preparation, frequency of injuries, severity of injuries, required precision of performance, energy expenditure, athletic intelligence, frequency of crucial moments, confrontation with opponents and, among other factors, the potential for fan abuse. When the relative rankings were totaled, PGA Tour golf finished in 11th place out of 14 jobs, beating only marathoners, bronco riders and hockey goalies.

It's impossible to argue that the athletic demands on a golfer even approach those of a boxer, pro quarterback and Olympic decathlete—the three jobs found toughest in the survey. However, golf ranked at the top in a surprising number of individual categories. It tied for the top spot in required precision of complexity of skill preparation, and complexity of the game. Only one other sport, boxing, matched it in the proximity of fans watching the athlete perform. And as one sports psychologist said, golf, more than any other sport, forces players to "slide in and out of concentration. It's a game in which emotions are a tremendous detriment."

While it's clear that there are differences between golf and other sports, it isn't completely clear whether ability in other sports does much for a golfer, and whether or not skills learned in another game are transferable to the links. One believer is Larry Nelson, a fine schoolboy basketball and baseball player in Georgia who had major college scholarship offers before blowing out his pitching arm. Nelson didn't take up golf until his 20s, after a tour of duty in Vietnam.

"The same muscle groups and mentality that go into being a good shooter in basketball are involved in good golf shots," Nelson contends. "Anyone who's been a good free-throw shooter should be a fairly good putter."

J. C. Snead agrees with Nelson, to a point. An exceptional all-round athlete in high school—he took all-State honors in three sports—Snead spent four years in the Washington Senators farm system as an outfielder before turning to professional golf. "The touch and feel aspect of these other sports is similar to what you find in golf's short game," he observes, "but I was a great free-throw shooter, had all the confidence in the world and seldom missed. Now my golf career would have been a whole lot more successful if I could have putted better. For years I didn't understand why I wasn't a better putter."

An ophthalmologist finally gave Snead some insight. "In basketball you're looking straight at your target, but in golf you're lining it up from the side," Snead says. "And the eye doctor explained that I have an astigmatism, which means I don't see things as they really are."

Over time, Snead has compensated for his visual disability with natural athletic skill and says non-athletes would do better to learn solid fundamentals and stick with them. "A real coordinated athlete who starts playing poorly will try to make corrections that will get him into bigger problems," Snead says. "But take a guy like Scott Simpson, who looks kind of mechanical but does the same thing all the time. Apologies to Scott, because I don't know if he was or wasn't an all-around athlete, but he looks more like a plodder than a natural. But what he does has made him a great golfer."

# An American Sport Revs Up[4]

*THE AMERICAN ENTERPRISE*, SEPTEMBER/OCTOBER 1999

Almost 35 years ago, *Esquire* magazine sent writer Tom Wolfe to Hamptonville, North Carolina, to look up a moonshine-runner-turned-stock-car-driver named Junior Johnson. Wolfe went back to New York with a story about men who drove so fast that (with no seat belts) they had to hang onto the steering wheel just to keep from flying out of the car. It was a tale of how the rural Southern code of honor and bravery produced the most daring men in sports, men who exhibited a physical courage extinct in most other parts of American society.

Today, the National Association of Stock Car Racing (NASCAR) is a $2 billion-a-year industry and the nation's most popular spectator sport. Junior Johnson still represents the "good old boy" tradition that gives NASCAR much of its flair, but a new champion named Jeff Gordon symbolizes what racing has become.

A clean-cut, photogenic, Christian conservative, Gordon is often compared to Michael Jordan in his appeal. *Forbes* labeled him the "hottest jock in the hottest sport in America" and "the next Michael Jordan of marketing" in 1998, after Gordon's product endorsements totaled $8.3 million. That didn't count the $9 million he won for driving.

"I'm seeing more and more children saying, 'When I grow up I want to be a race car driver,'" Gordon told *TAE*'s John Meroney. "That used to never happen. It was always, 'I want to be a baseball, basketball, or football player.' So I think we're definitely becoming more mainstream." Gordon notes that the strikes and salary disputes plaguing other sports are definitely not NASCAR's style.

Auto racing is winning new fans despite finding itself on the firing lines of political correctness. There's nothing environmentally chic about this gasgulping sport. The elite media (most recently, *Time*) like to strain to see racism in this heavily Southern pastime. And the circuit's championship—the Winston Cup—is, horrors, named after a cigarette. R. J. Reynolds pays more than $30 million a year to have its brand cited.

Junior Johnson is responsible for that. In 1971, he went to executives in Winston-Salem and asked whether they wanted to underwrite racing. Now he sees Washington's war on tobacco as an issue

4. Reprinted with permission from *The American Enterprise*, a national magazine of politics, business, and culture.



David Lundstrom was a standout basketball at Bradley University. And yet, he can only wish that Nelson's theory on the correlation between basketball and golf was true. "Golf was a lot harder for me than basketball," Lundstrom says. "In college, my golf scoring average was about a 78, and that was on easy courses. At the age of 22, I was still an 80s shooter. I had to practice like crazy for eight years to come close to qualifying. I don't think golf is even a little bit natural for me."

While multi-sport stars may struggle at golf, scrubs can just as easily excel. Consider the likes of Hubert Green. The two-time major champion may look slim and trim and athletic, but in truth is a self-professed klutz. "Man, I didn't have the agility, mobility or hostility for other sports," Green concedes. And though he loves basketball, Green says his vertical leap would barely clear a rural phone book. Oddly enough those deficiencies make him appreciate his golf skills even more.

***While multi-sport stars may struggle at golf, scrubs can just as easily excel.***

"I've played golf with Michael Jordan, Jerry Rice and Johnny Bench," Green says, "and I know they wish they could play golf like a pro. Bench is a very good player. But the tour level is different. And golf is so different from team sports, because when you screw up out here, there's no one to blame but yourself."

Unless, of course, you listen to Laoretti. "It's the reason that we hire caddies," he confides with a chuckle. "We can blame them for mistakes."

Bearing sole responsibility for your place in the game—not to mention your paycheck—is a major differentiation between golf and most other sports. The "Toughest Job" ranking even included a category called "Lack of Opportunity to Rationalize Failure." It's not that golfers don't try to blame a poor performance on bad lies, unlucky bounces or an opponent's annoying caddie, but like tennis players or boxers, they're pretty much on their own.

What's more, the mental side of the game is a punishing thing indeed. "Playing college basketball probably helped develop some mental toughness that I can draw on to shake off bad shots," Lundstrom says. "But when I had an off-night of shooting in basketball, I could do other things to have a good game and help the team win. I could rebound, set a tough pick, play tougher defense and dive for loose balls." In golf, hustling won't necessarily help your score.

While emotions can be detrimental, they often smolder just below the surface in professional golf. Hale Irwin, a two-time All Big Eight defensive back at the University of Colorado, found bliss in knocking opposing receivers on their backs. When he hits a 4-iron stiff to the pin and shatters the will of his competitor, the same attitude surely exists, although he'd never show it. Most golfers don't woof.

"Golf imposes a corral of civility around us," McCord says. "We have to control our primal instincts. But if I ever built a golf course, it would have punching bags waiting just past the 18th hole, so players could vent their feelings before going home."

While controlled aggression can be good for your game, the anger that's so useful in collision and contact sports such as football and basketball is a golfer's enemy, Snead says. "When someone knocks you on your ass in football," he says, "you've got a chance on the next play to find that guy and clock him. But in golf you're supposed to play the course and not the opponent. And anger over a bad shot leads to another bad shot and before you know it, you're out of the tournament. That's why pros try to control both anger and the urge to celebrate. It helps keep you on an even keel."

Balance, mental and physical, is the one thing common to golf and most other sports. "Balance and the transfer of weight is the critical issue," says Marsh, who grew up in family of exceptional athletes. "A good golf swing requires a weight transfer that's similar to a forehand in tennis, and what is called a cover drive in cricket. Great batsmen must hit a variety of shots, and so must golfers. And all great golfers have exceptional balance and hand-eye coordination."

Gary Player's famous post-swing lurch might seem the exception to the rule, but as Laoretti explains, "even the guys with the more unusual swings still have good balance. They've got their weight where its supposed to be at impact."

Like all other golfers, Laoretti has heard his share of jibes about the alleged simplicity of hitting a ball that's not hurtling about. "What a lot of folks shouldn't dismiss is that the static nature of the resting golf ball—especially when faced by a player who is also trying to remain still before swinging—can make things more difficult," he says. "In tennis you're moving before returning a serve; in baseball you're wiggling the bat; you're bouncing in a rhythm before passing a football."

Marsh adds, "Maybe the most perplexing difference between golf and other sports is that you're looking at the ball you're trying to hit, not at your target. You visualize your target, but you can't be looking at it and still strike the ball. It's somewhat unnatural."

Many golfers, however, are obviously athletes. "I'd challenge anyone who says golfers aren't athletic to watch Tiger Woods unleash on one drive, and tell me he's not a superior athlete," Marsh says.



| Below: The results of the author's research. In the left-hand column are 14 different jobs or positions in sports. Across the top are listed characteristics or skills required to perform each job adequately. Each sport is rated 1 to 5, 1 being the least, 5 being the maximum. Total scores are in the far right column. | Body coordination | Required precision of performance | Special physiological requirements | Special anatomical requirements | Need for physical preparation | Complexity of skill preparation | Energy expenditure | Complexity of the game | Athletic intelligence | Application of strategy | Opportunity for environmental distractions | Frequency of injuries | Severity of injuries | Degree of success | Proximity of the fans | Potential for fan abuse | Lack of opportunity to rationalize failure | Confrontation | Concentration time | Frequency of crucial moments | Total |
|---|---|---|---|---|---|---|---|---|---|---|---|---|---|---|---|---|---|---|---|---|---|
| Boxer | 3 | 2 | 5 | 2 | 5 | 5 | 5 | 4 | 5 | 4 | 1 | 4 | 5 | 3 | 5 | 5 | 5 | 5 | 3 | 4 | 80 |
| Pro quarterback | 3 | 2 | 2 | 4 | 2 | 4 | 2 | 5 | 5 | 5 | 4 | 5 | 4 | 5 | 3 | 5 | 3 | 4 | 3 | 3 | 73 |
| Decathlete | 5 | 5 | 5 | 5 | 5 | 5 | 5 | 5 | 4 | 2 | 3 | 2 | 1 | 3 | 1 | 1 | 5 | 2 | 5 | 4 | 73 |
| Basketball player | 5 | 3 | 5 | 5 | 4 | 4 | 4 | 4 | 5 | 3 | 1 | 3 | 3 | 2 | 4 | 4 | 2 | 4 | 2 | 2 | 68 |
| American soccer player | 5 | 3 | 4 | 2 | 4 | 4 | 4 | 4 | 5 | 3 | 3 | 3 | 3 | 2 | 3 | 2 | 2 | 4 | 2 | 2 | 64 |
| Downhill skier | 2 | 5 | 3 | 2 | 3 | 3 | 2 | 3 | 5 | 2 | 5 | 4 | 4 | 4 | 1 | 1 | 3 | 1 | 4 | 5 | 62 |
| Baseball catcher/hitter | 3 | 5 | 2 | 1 | 2 | 1 | 2 | 5 | 3 | 5 | 3 | 3 | 3 | 5 | 4 | 4 | 2 | 3 | 3 | 2 | 61 |
| Tennis player | 4 | 4 | 4 | 2 | 3 | 5 | 3 | 4 | 3 | 3 | 1 | 1 | 1 | 3 | 4 | 2 | 5 | 3 | 3 | 2 | 60 |
| Racecar driver | 1 | 4 | 1 | 1 | 1 | 3 | 4 | 4 | 5 | 3 | 5 | 2 | 5 | 5 | 1 | 1 | 1 | 2 | 5 | 5 | 59 |
| [illegible] | 4 | 5 | 3 | 4 | 3 | 5 | 2 | 3 | 1 | 1 | 3 | 1 | 1 | 3 | 4 | 1 | 3 | 1 | 4 | 4 | 56 |
| [illegible] | [illegible] | [illegible] | [illegible] | [illegible] | [illegible] | [illegible] | 1 | 5 | 4 | 3 | 4 | 1 | 1 | 4 | 5 | 2 | 3 | 2 | 3 | 2 | 55 |
| [illegible] | [illegible] | [illegible] | [illegible] | [illegible] | [illegible] | [illegible] | [illegible] | [illegible] | [illegible] | [illegible] | [illegible] | [illegible] | [illegible] | [illegible] | [illegible] | 5 | 3 | 3 | 2 | 3 | 53 |

of personal freedom. "I think Clinton's wrong with what he's doing on it," says Johnson. "I've never smoked, but I feel that if anybody's willing to give up his health for what he enjoys, that's his business and ain't a damn bit of anybody else's. It's the mentality of, 'We're going to fix the whole country.'"

Gordon, another non-smoker, is also unconcerned about the association with tobacco. He proudly recognized Reynolds when he won Daytona in February and calls Washington's attack on tobacco "a shame" that "the lawyers just won't let end."

Certainly Bill Clinton is no favorite in NASCAR territory. When he campaigned at the Southern 500 in 1992 he was met with intense chanting of "Draft dodger!" and "Go home, cheater!" Dale Earnhardt refused to give him a tour. "They should find someone else," said The Intimidator.

Contrast that reception to the one received by Ronald Reagan when he appeared at Daytona in 1984. Not only was Reagan welcomed into the winner's circle to help Richard Petty celebrate his 200th NASCAR Winston Cup victory, but the Gipper also went back to his sportscaster roots, calling part of the race with announcer Ned Jarrett. Afterward, he invoked the Founders: "From what I've read about Patrick Henry, he'd have been out on the track with one of the cars. The Founding Fathers were kind of gutsy, and we'd better not forget that."

Most stock car drivers instinctively share a traditional American view: Freedom and responsibility and risk are all interlinked. "They're straight-shooting guys," says GOP freshman Representative Robin Hayes, the only member of Congress who is part owner of a NASCAR team. Gordon represents the North Carolina district that includes Charlotte's famous Lowes Motor Speedway.

"A big part of racing is honesty," he explains. "There's a bad crash, a lot of damage is done . . . what's the explanation? 'That's racing.' No excuses. Nothing disingenuous. Never mind what the meaning of 'is' is. That doesn't fit. It's just a truthful, straightforward philosophy."

Gentlemen, start your engines.

# They Got More Than Just Game[5]

## Female Athletes Win Enormous Popularity

BY SARA HAMMEL AND ANNA MULRINE
*U.S. NEWS & WORLD REPORT,* JULY 12, 1999

True, at last week's U.S. versus Germany Women's World Cup soccer quarterfinal game in Landover, Md., the lines for ice cream were twice as long as those for beer. Legions of preteen "mini-Mias" were out in force, wearing the jersey of the sport's biggest star, No. 9 Mia Hamm, and going hoarse as they chanted "U-S-A!" But cheering elbow to elbow with them in the stands, bare chested with "You Goal, Girls!" painted on their backs, was a less touted but equally loyal group of fans: the guys.

"Women's soccer is just better than men's," says Ike Coles, 26, of Woodbridge, Va., tailgating with a bunch of his male friends before the game. "Quicker passes, more finesse. And," he notes proudly, "our women win." Adds Fabio Raimundo, 23, who flew from Sao Paulo, Brazil, to see the World Cup matches, "The American women have attitude. I love them."

Winning, attitude: just what fans—and advertisers—like to hear. Both are lining up behind women's soccer in force. The opening game on June 26, in which the United States trounced Denmark 3-0, drew 79,000 people—the largest crowd ever for a women's sporting event. Since then, U.S. matches have averaged 62,000 fans—not bad for an event whose governing board, FIFA, had to be persuaded by United States tournament officials and players that it would be able to fill big venues.

"When fans go to a women's sporting event," says Julie Foudy, cocaptain and star midfielder for the U.S. team, "they come away thinking, 'That was a great event.' There's entertainment value, there's something fresh, there's a lot of purity that's lacking on the men's side." And advertisers want to go where the boys are: Bruce Hudson, director of international sports marketing for Anheuser-Busch, an official sponsor of the Women's World Cup, says, "Obviously, we're not trying to appeal to young girls." The beer company targets its audience: "Males 21 to 34 are our largest demographic."

Aficionados argue that the women's game is more exciting than men's soccer. Women are more likely to have one-on-one confrontations, versus the long sweeping passes (and, say critics, less scintillating play) of the men. "The women are more offensive-minded," says Marla Messing, president of Women's World Cup Soccer. And it shows. "With men, you get those 0-0 ties," laments Coles, while the women's games have actually been high scoring: an average of four goals per match. The women's team has more than just talent; they've got personality, too, which other sports (think of tennis's Venus Williams or Martina Hingis) are also benefiting from.

**Dolls, Shoes, and Drinks.**

Big business is taking notice, too, which means that you can now buy Women's World Cup Barbie dolls. In addition to her ubiquitous Nike commercial, Mia Hamm has a big deal with Gatorade. Bob Williams, president of Burns Celebrity Sports Service, a Chicago

***Aficionados argue that the women's game is more exciting than men's soccer.***

sports agency, says that advertisers didn't believe in female athletes before the WNBA and this World Cup. Now there are stars like Chamique Holdsclaw, the University of Tennessee basketball phenom who recently signed with the Washington Mystics. After a shoe-company bidding war, Nike came through with a five-year contract and a signature Holdsclaw shoe. "Five years for a female athlete who hasn't bounced a basketball professionally is unheard of," says Williams.

These women didn't turn into star athletes overnight, nor did they do it without a sea change in the way culture viewed the role of sports in their lives. They are the first generation that, at an early age, had the resources, training, and encouragement they needed to excel at their chosen sport. "From the first time they kicked a ball," notes Williams, "there have been leagues, and teams, and instruction." Sports professionals credit Title IX, enacted in 1972 to prohibit sex discrimination at educational institutions receiving federal funds, with providing the crucial guarantees. Once schools were forced to provide teams and scholarship money for women and girls, a farm system for female athletes slowly kicked into gear. The result is that today 1 in 3 girls is playing organized sports, up from 1 in 27 before Title IX. This, in turn, has spawned skilled athletes equipped for professional sports and an enormous base of little girls to worship them. "People don't realize it takes 10 to 15 years to make a professional athlete," says

Donna Lopiano, executive director of the Women's Sports Foundation. Another major factor was the 1996 Olympics, which saw record participation and achievement by women.

**No Parity Yet**

Gains in popularity have yet to be matched fully in pay. At Wimbledon this year, although the women's games generated much more excitement, tournament officials ignored players' lobbying for equal pay (the female winner will pocket 83 percent of what the male will). "We have a long, long way to go," says tennis great Billie Jean King. "We need sponsors who believe in the . . . soccer pro leagues. We need women [executives] who believe in women's tennis to understand there's a vision, that they'll really get a bang for their buck."

No one can be sure where the phenomenon will go from here—if more corporate sponsors will jump on board for the long haul, if talk of a professional soccer league will turn into reality, or if solid TV ratings will attract still more TV coverage (only 6 percent of televised sports are women's). Hudson of Anheuser-Busch will meet this week before the July 10 Los Angeles final with a committee that is discussing the viability of a professional American women's soccer league. He says it has a shot, since "we've seen a lot more personalities coming forward" in the World Cup events.

Personalities that are now more widely accepted. Babe Didrikson Zaharias, considered by many to be the best athlete of all time, won two gold medals in track events at the 1932 Olympics and helped form the LPGA, the oldest professional women's tour, in 1949. She was a true celebrity, but along with adulation she faced accusations that she wasn't feminine enough, notes Mariah Burton Nelson, a former Stanford University basketball player and author of *Embracing Victory*. "It used to be you had to wear a skirt and not touch anyone else, stay on your own side of the net. Now you have big, strong sweaty women knocking each other down . . . and thrilling fans."

# Tennis Racket[6]

BY PATRICK HRUBY
*INSIGHT ON THE NEWS*, MAY 22, 2000

Trash talk and saucy rivalries. Short skirts and taut thighs. Juicy gossip and endless melodrama. With its colorful cast and sudsy story lines, women's tennis isn't just different—it's an unpredictable, irresistible cocktail of jest, pathos and killer top-spin.

The Women's Tennis Association, or WTA, is booming: Ratings are up; attendance has increased four years running. Players such as teen tennis queen Anna Kournikova have become crossover stars. In November, the WTA signed a title sponsorship pact with Sara Lee subsidiary Sanex worth as much as $45 million—the largest deal in the history of women's sports.

"Everyone is excited to watch, to see what's going to happen next, to see who is going to go where," says its defending U.S. Open champion Serena Williams. "It's the future."

If women's tennis is the future, then tomorrow owes a debt to Hollywood producer Aaron Spelling. Consider the off court intrigue at the recent Ericsson Open, which featured everything save a special guest appearance by actress Heather Locklear:

- Venus Williams, a U.S. Open finalist in 1997 and sister to Serena, purportedly was considering retirement at age 19—the better to pursue a career in fashion design.
- Jennifer Capriati, tennis' prodigal daughter, was smiling again, reputedly due to her new boyfriend, fellow pro Xavier Malisse.
- Kournikova was rumored to have a new boyfriend as well, Ecuadorian tennis star Nicolas Lapentti, dashing earlier speculation that she planned to use the tournament to publicly announce a long-suspected engagement to forward Pavel Bure of the National Hockey League's Florida Panthers.

"Every day there's something different going on," says Alexandra Stevenson, "different boyfriends and girlfriends, all these different characters. I don't know if any other sports have so many interesting facts every day. It makes a great story."

---

So does Stevenson, for that matter. Making her pro debut last year at Wimbledon, she became the first female qualifier in the tournament's history to reach the semifinals—an achievement nearly overshadowed by the media tizzy surrounding the identity of her father, National Basketball Association Hall of Famer Julius Erving.

Also tweaking the London tabloids was fellow semifinalist Mirjana Lucic, who fled Croatia a year earlier while accusing her father of abuse, and quarterfinalist Jelena Dokic, who found herself defending her overbearing coach/father, Damir, after a drunken rage got him thrown into jail.

Then there are the game's colorful leading ladies:

- Martina Hingis, dubbed the "most attention-loving, endorsement-snatching, trash-talking No. 1 player in the history of women's tennis" by *Tennis* magazine;
- former champion Monica Seles, battling back from the death of her father and a brutal on-court stabbing in April 1993;
- onetime teen phenom Capriati, rebuilding both her game and her life after dallying with drugs and burnout.

This is not to overlook current No. 1 ranked Lindsay Davenport, whose down-to-earth normalcy throws the whole dizzying collage into sharp relief. "It's very important to have personalities that bring people into the sport," Davenport says. "The men are maybe playing their best tennis ever, but they really only have Pete Sampras and Andre Agassi drawing people. I think we have a great mix of players."

Not to mention a slew of catty, bratty rivalries fueled by smack talk that would make Gary Payton blush. At last year's U.S. Open, Hingis and the Williams sisters engaged in a frothy verbal tit for tat. Hingis also tossed barbs at lesbian opponent Amelie Mauresmo during the 1999 Australian Open, calling her "half a man."

"People in any sport are more interested in watching the great players who are charismatic and have personality," says Bart McGuire, women's tour chief executive officer. "Conflicting styles and conflicting personalities add interest to the game."

So does sex appeal. From Steffi Graf's appearance in *Sports Illustrated's* swimsuit issue, to Hingis' vampy star turn on the cover of *GQ*, to Kournikova's outfit at a recent tour awards banquet—6 inch heels, black miniskirt, translucent top, leopard-print bra—many of the tour's biggest names hardly are shy about sharing their, um, assets. (Among the 14 tips given to ballboys at the Ericsson Open, No. 7 instructs, "Do not stare at Anna Kournikova.")

"We make no apologies for having women who are very attractive on the tour," McGuire says. "With movie actors and actresses, would you consider it inappropriate to have attractive women and men in the business? Clearly not. It's a plus there, and it's a plus for us."

That plus has triggered a NASDAQ type boom for the sport. In 1999, the WTA set an attendance record for the fourth consecutive year, drawing a record 3.9 million spectators to its 57 tournaments worldwide, a 13 percent increase from 1998. Likewise, overall U.S. television ratings for nine tournament finals in 1999 were up 38 percent. This year the tour has added five new events and an additional $3 million in prize money, while January's Australian Open final (matching Davenport and Hingis) was ESPN's most viewed women's tennis telecast ever and the sixth most-viewed tennis telecast in the network's history.

**_"We make no apologies for having women who are very attractive on the tour."—_**
**Bart McGuire, women's tour chief executive.**

"The Women's World Cup soccer sold out the Rose Bowl and obtained better ratings than the NBA," McGuire recalls. "A few days later, the WNBA All-Star game sold out Madison Square Garden. The impact of all that, culminating in our extraordinary ratings at the U.S. Open and the extraordinary coverage we created, kind of broke the logjam. Far more people were willing to put money on the table for us."

The players have profited, too, needless to say. Last year, Venus Williams signed deals with American Express and Wilson. Hingis, who also endorses shampoo and fruit juices, agreed to a five-year clothing deal with Adidas that pays an estimated $2 million annually. Davenport became Nike's highest-paid female athlete with a reported five-year, $11 million contract.

"There seems to be more money for more players," Seles says. "Before, if you weren't No. 1 or No. 2 in the world, there weren't too many opportunities off court. Now there seems to be four or five players who are doing much better earning-wise off-court than on-court."

Tops among them is Kournikova, who resides in an endorsement neighborhood all her own. Though she has yet to win a tour title, the pouty-upped star has contracts with Adidas (clothes), Yonex (racquet), Berlei (sports bra), Namco (video game) and Charles Schwab (financial services) worth more than a combined $10 million a year, making her the tour leader in off-court earnings.

"There have been beautiful tennis players before, but if they didn't do something people forgot about them," says tennis historian Bud Collins. "But here's a woman who's never done anything, never won anything and she's maybe the best-known player in all of tennis. That's a phenomenon. And a player like Kournikova drags the rest of the tour with her."

Despite all this success, there's concern within the sport that its popularity remains cyclical and its impressive gains have been purchased with the shaky credit of celebrity. "When you start relying on the players to sell your tickets, that only works when the players are hot," says John Korff, WTA board member and tournament director for the A&P Classic. "You get lucky that you have a Kournikova or the Williams sisters. But you never know when you're not going to have them. And then what are you going to do? You have to do something to make your event bigger than the players."

Korff and others have reason to be a bit concerned. Venus Williams actually may retire. Kournikova's sports management group, Octagon, is working to tone down her sultry image. And while the tour busily touts its next generation—last year, the tour had 15 new tournament winners, compared with six in 1998—there's no telling if the new guard will have the current crop's colorful appeal.

Moreover, some players worry that the tour's personality push may end up downgrading its level of play. "It's great to see women athletes getting on the cover of *Forbes*," Seles says. "I just hope it won't put the emphasis on young girls starting out that say, 'Gee, I want to play tennis because I'm going to make all these millions of dollars.' It still should be for the love of the game."

For now, however, don't expect the WTA to alter its marketing pitch. According to McGuire, promoting the tour's human-interest stories is the best way to ensure the game's ongoing popularity "The audiences that we want to attract go beyond the rabid tennis fan and even beyond the rabid sports fan," he says. "You want to attract the same people who will tune into the finals of the Masters because Tiger Woods is playing. They may not watch golf much for the rest of the year, but for the compelling tournaments, for the compelling stories, they will."

## Stargazing: A Guide to the WTA Galaxy

### PLANET LOVETRON: Anna Kournikova

From her provocative posters to her predilection for 6-inch heels, the self-proclaimed virgin is the WTA's resident *objet d'amour*, a seemingly inexhaustible source of tabloid fodder. Reportedly engaged to Florida Panthers forward Pavel Bure, she has been spotted kissing tennis hunk Mark Philippoussis and has been linked with Ecuadorian tennis player Nicolas Lapentti as well as Brazilian soccer star Ronaldo and Detroit Red Wings forward Sergei Fedorov.

### TOTAL ECLIPSE?: Venus and Serena

With her overpowering serve and unmatched athletic ability, 19-year-old Venus Williams long has been tabbed the future of women's tennis. But her younger sister, Serena, became the first Williams to win a Grand Slam event by capturing last year's U.S. Open.

### COMET CAPRIATI: Jennifer Capriati

Like Valley's Comet, Capriati keeps coming back. After four years in the WTA top 10, then-17-year-old Capriati dropped off the tour in 1993, citing burnout and fatigue. The next year, she was arrested in a sleazy Florida motel and charged with marijuana possession. But Capriati rebounded in 1999, winning two tournaments and raising her ranking from No. 101 to No. 23.

### THE DADDY NEBULAE: Mary Pierce, Alexandra Stevenson, Mirjana Lucic, Jelena Dokic

Daddy dearest? Not for this cluster of stars. Pierce long has shared a troubled relationship with her father, Jim, who was banned from the grounds of WTA tournaments after a series of outbursts. Dokic's father, Damir, overimbibed at an English tournament, got thrown out and later was arrested. Lucic says her father abused her. And Stevenson has almost no contact with her father, NBA Hall of Famer Julius Erving.

### TEEN-AGE SUPERNOVA: Martina Hingis

Hingis, the youngest player to win a Grand Slam title in the open era and the youngest top-ranked player in WTA tour history, is a smack-spewing, endorsement-hogging, titlewinning teen terror, limited only by her own adolescent angst. After losing in unsportsmanlike fashion to Steffi Graf in the 1999 French Open final, she threw a petulant fit, feuded with her mother and coach, then tanked in the first round of Wimbledon.

### LOST IN (ANDRE'S) SPACE: Steffi Graf

Before her retirement last August, the stoic Graf was known more for her on-court dominance than her off-court life. But that changed at the 1999 U.S. Open final, where she was seen cheering Andre Agassi from the stands. Now firmly locked in a love orbit around the most charismatic player on the men's tour, Graf forms the fairer half of tennis' top couple.

### DOWN TO EARTH: Lindsay Davenport

Three years, three Grand Slam titles and the current No.1 ranking: One might expect at least a little arrogance from Davenport. But unlike most of her younger rivals, the 23-year-old is stunningly normal: She doesn't talk trash, has a good relationship with her parents and has yet to make headlines through bratty behavior.

### LONELY PLANET MONICA SELES

In the early 1990s, Seles owned the tour, winning nine Grand Slams between 1990 and 1993. Since then, it has been tragedy and heartbreak: A deranged fan stabbed her in 1993; she lost her beloved father/coach, Karolj, to cancer in 1998.

# II. Youth Sports

PhotoDisc

# *Editor's Introduction*

Parents have been troubled in recent years by reports that greater numbers of their children are overweight, that young people spend more time in front of the television than they do outside playing, and that their sedentary lifestyle will result in a variety of health problems as they grow to adulthood. To rectify the situation—or to prevent its occurrence altogether—many of these parents encourage their children to participate in organized sports, including Little League, baseball, soccer, or hockey, to name but a few. They shuttle their boys and girls to practices and meets and, anxious to share in their children's experiences or bask in their glory, often remain to watch them play, shouting encouragement or criticism from the sidelines. If their experience playing sports is positive, these children will not only become physically fit but will also learn the kinds of valuable lessons about life of which Jeff Kemp speaks (see Section I). For too many children, however, the experience of participating in youth sports will be spoiled by injury or the attitudes and behavior of coaches and parents. Section II looks at these and other important issues concerning youth sports in America today.

The section begins with an example of youth sports at its most edifying. Kerry Pianoforte's article "Challenger Baseball: A League of Their Own" introduces readers to a place where fun is the top priority and children with special needs, such as those with autism, can learn "concentration and focus, as well as . . . good sportsmanship." Nevertheless, despite the many benefits to children who participate in youth sports, problems can arise when the games and their results assume an inordinate significance in the lives of parents and children. Debra Galant's article "As American As Volvos and Rovers" describes the complicated world of suburban youth soccer, which some fear has become "professionalized" by the introduction of traveling teams and a "rigorous tryout process." When 6- and 7-year-olds are expected to show enough promise to become future stars of the fledgling Major League Soccer teams, what many believe is an unreasonable amount of pressure is placed on children to perform and parents to support them, financially and emotionally. Unfortunately, many parents go too far in demonstrating that support, as William Nack and Lester Munson report in "Out of Control." In recent years, young people have watched helplessly as their parents have killed each other over disputes arising during practice sessions or attacked coaches on the field during games to express their displeasure with a call or decision. The effects on the children who witness such behavior run the gamut from embarrassment to horror, prompting many of these young people to quit organized sports completely.

Every year, many youths are forced to abandon athletic competition due to repeat injuries, a situation discussed by Jeffrey H. Tyler and Michael E. Nelson in "Second Impact Syndrome: Sports Confront Consequences of Concussions." The writers present a number of cautionary tales for coaches and parents inclined to dismiss the head injuries suffered by young people during games, injuries that result in death about 50% of the time. According to Tyler and Nelson, more schools and recreational organizations are adopting stricter guidelines to ensure the safety of young players, but parents and players need to be further educated about the dangers of second impact syndrome as well.

# Challenger Baseball

## A League of Their Own[1]

BY KERRY PIANOFORTE
*EXCEPTIONAL PARENT,* MAY 2000

Seven-year-old Bonnie was part of the Oradell, NJ, Challenger Baseball League all season. Bonnie, who is virtually non-verbal and does not have a diagnosis, never showed any outward sign she was even getting anything out of the weekly games. Then, on the second-to-last game of the season, as one of the players hit a ground ball, Bonnie broke away from her mother, picked up the ball and threw it to first base. According to Challenger coach Terri Del Greco, "We screamed, we cheered and cried. It was just so wonderful." Accomplishments like Bonnie's are what makes Challenger League the success it is today.

**Baseball for All**

Founded 10 years ago, Challenger League is a division of Little League baseball. It is designed to allow children with physical and mental disabilities to participate and benefit from playing baseball. Challenger League is a fun and effective way to get children with special needs involved in sports in a non-competitive setting. Each Challenger team consists of 8-12 players. Each player has a buddy who helps him or her. Buddies help players hit the ball, run the bases, and pay attention while they are in the field. The buddies can either be volunteers from local schools or parents. Terri's husband, Steven, coaches, and older son, David, 16, is involved in the games as well. Terri says, "Sometimes there are more people on the field than there are in the stands. The majority of the kids need one-on-one attention."

Children can either hit from a tee-ball stand or be pitched to by a coach. The entire team gets up to bat each inning and no score is taken. The focus is on having a good time and allowing each child to challenge his or her abilities. The teams play other local teams and travel to play games in neighboring towns. Terri notes, "It is fun for the kids to travel, see other towns, and meet new kids. They remember each other from year to year."

---

1. Article by Kerry Pianoforte from *Exceptional Parent* May 2000. 

### Catching Challenger Fever

Terri found out about Challenger after reading about a league in a neighboring town. She felt that her son Stevie, who has autism, would benefit from the stimulation. Stevie, then 7, had never participated in sports before, so Terri signed him up. Through her research Terri learned that all Little Leagues are chartered to have a Challenger division. Then she began working to form a Challenger team for her own town for the next season.

According to Terri, "I was motivated because this was something that I wanted to do for my son. I also felt that this would be something that would be good for the town." Terri says the local Little League was very supportive. In the first season, Terri's Oradell division had one team. The following year, however, so many more children signed up that they started a second team. By the fourth year a third team was added. Roger Hoffman, a coach for one of the new teams and the father of a son who has a disability says, "As parents of a child who has special needs, we are always looking to broaden his experiences and to participate in mainstream activities."

Terri credits the League's rapid expansion mainly to old-fashioned word of mouth. In addition to parents spreading the word, Terri also sends out press releases every year. She leaves flyers at the school's Child Study Team offices in towns that she is targeting and asks the staff to give the information to family's for whom Challenger League would be appropriate.

### Fun Is the Name of the Game

Terri sees many benefits for children with special needs who participate in Challenger League. "They're getting fresh air, they're getting exercise, and they're getting social opportunity by meeting different children. They are being visible in the community, which is important," she remarks. The children have a chance to have fun with friends and family and "fun is the name of the game. If we're not having a good time, then why are we here?"

Perseverance is also a major ingredient to success. Terri advises, "You cannot give up too soon. You do not know what these kids are capable of. You may have to slug it out for two or more years before it clicks. But when you see them doing it, it is definitely worth it."

### Skills, Accomplishments, and Fun

Baseball teaches many important skills that are useful both on and off the field. The children learn turn taking and following directions, they improve their concentration and focus, as well as learn good sportsmanship. These are all skills that will benefit them in real life situations.

Challenger coach Roger Hoffman notes, "The biggest change that we see in the kids is their enthusiasm for the game as the years go by. When we first started, no one was able to hit the ball, much less field. Today, everyone on the team hits from pitching and we are able to run some simple plays." It is these kind of accomplishments that parents and coaches cherish. Terri's son Stevie has moderate to severe, late onset autism and sensory processing issues. Terri says, "My son has a lot going on. For him to get up there and hit a pitched ball and to run to first base all by himself is a big accomplishment. We are very proud."

The sense of acceptance and easy-going pace of Challenger League helps everyone have a good time. Flexibility and a sense of humor are a must. Terri recalls a particular game when her son was digging up the bases while out on the field. He dislodged first base and walked off the field with it. Terri recalls with a laugh, "One of the other parents remarked, 'Well, in this league when we talk about stealing bases, we really mean stealing bases!'"

There has been a growth in Challenger Leagues throughout the state. Terri feels that improved communications among the local town's Challenger Leagues has helped. Lou Verile, the founder of the Bergenfield League, was recently appointed to be the New Jersey advisor for Challenger League. Two years ago, he organized a meeting and they decided to have a Fun Day. This proved to be an effective way for the teams to meet each other, to raise awareness in the community, and of course, it would be a fun day for the children. Through the cooperation of all the leagues, who solicited donations from local merchants, Fun Day was a huge success. The children played games and received gifts. As a result, Fun Day has become an annual event and has helped the local Challenger Leagues meet and trade information. Terri says, "There is enormous benefit to the parents because we get to meet and network. We know there is no one book written to tell you where the schools, camps, sports, and programs are. Parents have the knowledge."

**Starting a Challenger League**

For parents who want to start a Challenger League in their area, Terri advises going to their local Little League and finding out whether there are any Challenger Leagues in their district. If not, parents can start recruiting for their own league at their child's school. Word of mouth is one of the most effective ways to get a message across. It may also be beneficial to enlist the help of some regular Little League members. These baseball veterans can offer help and guidance in coaching a successful team and gaining community support.

Challenger League is a great opportunity for children who have special needs to learn a sport and have some much needed fun. It also offers parents and children a unique bonding experience that they may not have in their day-to-day lives. The benefits to the players are many so why not get out there on the field and batter up!

# As American As Volvos and Rovers[2]

BY DEBRA GALANT
*NEW YORK TIMES,* DECEMBER 5, 1999

The suburban soccer match, it can be argued, is the modern equivalent of the square dance. It is the weekly gathering place where people stand around, watch other people move vigorously, hoot, clap—and, of course, gossip.

The soccer field has become such an "in" place that mothers have been known to sign up reluctant kickers just so they won't miss out on their Saturday mornings along the sidelines with like-minded mothers.

"It's a sociological thing, says Gloria Averbuch (pronounced AY-ver-bush), a soccer mom here who helped write *Goal!: The Ultimate Guide for Soccer Moms and Dads* (Rodale Press, $15.95). "It's really a family movement."

But dig a little deeper and you discover pockets of resentment and layers of contradiction. "Soccer people are so obnoxious," said one parent whose son plays football. "They say the rest of the world loves soccer. Well, the rest of the world uses the metric system, too. If the rest of the world is so great and we're so lousy, how come the rest of the world is beating down our doors to get in?"

For a sport whose most obvious American fans are immigrants, it seems to have achieved its most passionate following among the Eddie Bauer set.

Though all you need to play are cleats, shin pads and a ball, at the highest levels parents spend thousands of dollars sending their progeny to far-flung tournaments and elite soccer camps. Moreover, soccer attracts young players because it is easy to learn and rarely puts children on the spot.

"One of the great things about soccer is there's no such thing as right field," says Mike May, spokesman for the Sporting Good Manufacturers Association.

Yet with the rise of traveling leagues, this seemingly simple sport has become the most recent metaphor for the stresses and competitiveness of childhood.

---

2. Article by Debra Galant from *New York Times* December 5, 1999. 

Increasingly, it is becoming a battleground for the future of professional spectator sports in this country. And just as the major leagues compete at the box office and on television for the loyalty of their fans, so too do the various youth sports compete at the local level over scarce playing fields.

In the ethnically diverse town of Clifton—next to the soccer-crazed town of Montclair—there are mixed emotions about the rise in popularity of soccer. With a large immigrant community, it boasts the second-ranked high school soccer team in the country. But Clifton's high school football team—once a dynasty in the state—is struggling.

"There's a historical sense over the years of being a strong football town," said Al Greco, Clifton's director of human services, who oversees recreation. "But that's changing."

Chet Parlavecchio, who was brought in this fall to turn around the failing football program at Clifton High School, contends that "football's still the No. 1 sport" in just about every town in America.

"The state championship soccer game is never going to outdraw the state championship football game," said Mr. Parlavecchio.

Indeed, Clifton's nationally ranked soccer team draws at most a few hundred fans to a game, while its football team, which won only one game this season, regularly draws 1,500 to 2,000, said Bill Cannici, the school's principal.

But if soccer is making a steady advance in places like Clifton and Montclair, it has not aroused much enthusiasm in the inner cities, where there are fewer playing fields or money to support a traveling team.

Clearly, soccer's time has come among the children of suburbia. According to 1999 statistics provided by the sporting goods manufacturers, soccer is the second-ranked team sport among children ages 6 to 11 (after basketball), and the third-ranked team sport among youths 12 to 17 (after basketball and volleyball).

"The figures are staggering, 18 million participants," said Ashley Hammond, who wrote *Goal!: The Ultimate Guide for Soccer Moms and Dads* with Ms. Averbuch

Soccer fans tick off myriad reasons for the game's increasing popularity. It seems safe; young children can play; girls can succeed; it requires more physical activity than other sports. Plus, there's a worldly quality to the sport that attracts the Birkenstock-and-granola set—even those who have rebelled against the jock mindset since their first pair of thick eyeglasses.

At the basic level, at least, everybody is invited to try. And it certainly does not hurt that the term "soccer mom" was the most memorable phrase of the 1996 Presidential election. The 1990's incarnation of American motherhood may work full time and buy birthday cakes at Carvel, but at least she gets her child to soccer practice on time in the family Volvo or Land Rover.

Some soccer enthusiasts describe their sport in terms usually reserved for poetry, or love. "It resembles ballet in some respects," said Mr. Hammond. "It's a beautiful thing."

But Dick Barnes, co-author of *The Soccer Mom Handbook* (Sports Barn, 1997), believes that the recent soccer boom has to some extent been fueled with the angst of baby boomer parents. "The yuppie factor of wanting the best for their kids, the whole evolution of society toward more organized activities for kids, with more parents both working, you're scheduling things for kids," Mr. Barnes said. "You don't just give them a ball and send them down to the playground and tell them to come back at dinner."

***Clearly, soccer's time has come among the children of suburbia.***

What is interesting, however, is that the success of soccer may also carry the seeds of its own decline.

There was one troubling statistic in the survey done by the Sporting Good Manufacturers Association: participation among youths 6 to 11 had declined 9 percent from the previous survey.

It is the rise of the traveling team—an elite squad chosen after a long selection process, which practices frequently and travels to games as far as an hour away—that has recently split the soccer community and may account for some attrition. The travel team has prospered because people like Mr. Hammond, a former soccer player in England, have "professionalized" the children's sport.

"The boom time occured in the early 90's for our companies," Mr. Hammond said. "We took a weekend recreational sport in this country and turned it into a 7-day-a-week, 52-week-of-the-year sport."

Soccer can be played into the evening and year-round here in Mr. Hammond's Soccer Domain, a full-size soccer field under an inflatable bubble that was built this year by Steve Plofker, a lawyer and developer here.

The 34-year-old Mr. Hammond, known as Ash, came to this country in the late 1980's, when "there was really no industry here at the time." He said he approached the Montclair United Soccer Club with a "vision" of what youth soccer could be "What I was selling," he said, "was the availability of my time at 4 o'clock."

Mr. Hammond's pitch amounted to a kind of revolution in youth sports, which have historically been coached by the fathers of team members—meaning that practices and games had to revolve around work schedules squeezed in during the last light of daylight saving time. When professionals like Mr. Hammond became available, soccer joined the pantheon of after-school activities to compete for time with piano, dance, art and even religious instruction. In the process, it also became a big business.

With professional coaching, young soccer players are also better and more competitive. Travelling soccer leagues were developed, with "flights" for players of differing abilities. Soccer academies were developed to further winnow out the best and the fastest. At its highest levels, each state, including New Jersey, runs its own Olympic Development Program to identify the sport's most promising young athletes. These players, as young as 12, begin taking airplanes—rather than minivans—to soccer matches

Then there are those youthful aspirations.

***The travel team has prospered because people . . . have "professionalized" the children's sport.***

Major League Soccer, the newest incarnation of professional soccer in this country, was organized four years ago. Team owners include Lamar Hunt; John Kluge, chairman of Metromedia Company; and Phil Anschutz, chairman of Qwest Communications. The commissioner, Don Garber, who began in September, was previously a marketing executive with the National Football League, and his mission is nothing less than to turn soccer into a major spectator sport in this country.

It is a goal that has been tried before. Children played organized soccer in this country in the 1970's, and even then, soccer afficionados argued that when these children grew up they would turn the United States into a nation of rabid soccer fans. It never happened. The last professional league—the North American Soccer League—ran from 1970 to 1984.

And except for the recent Women's World Cup that America [won] in a thrilling overtime victory against China, most Americans have greeted the beloved global pastime with a yawn. "This is the last kick of the can for professional soccer in this country," Mr. Garber admitted.

For now, the growth of soccer in the 1990's outshadows anything that has ever happened on this country's playing fields, and that is making the National Football League edgy. The league recently committed $100 million over the next seven years to expand youth football in this country.

But for soccer to ultimately succeed, several things must happen. The children and parents who mob suburban soccer fields on weekends have to start watching professional soccer on television and at stadiums. And the United States has to win a men's World Soccer Cup. Toward that end, the United States Soccer Federation, which governs all levels of the sport in this country, has developed a plan to try to capture the World Cup by 2010.

Mr. Garber says the traveling soccer leagues, the "academies," and the Olympic Development Programs are a crucial link. "It's an absolutely necessity," he says.

Yet along the way, traveling soccer has developed its critics. Among them is Julie Ross, whose 7-year-old son, Max, failed to make the team in Glen Ridge last summer. At the time Mrs. Ross thought her son was a little young for such competition but allowed him to try because he liked soccer so much and because one of his best friends was trying out too.

His friend made the team; Max didn't.

"Max didn't take it well," Mrs. Ross said. "He kept saying it wasn't fair."

Although Max went on to play in the town's recreational league this fall, he was discouraged further by the fact that his team had no traveling players, and consistently lost to the other teams, which did.

There is an end-of-the-game-ritual in many youth sports, including soccer, in which the players from both teams form lines, slap hands and say, "good game" in the spirt of sportsmanship. By the end of the season, however, Max was saying "bad game" instead. "It's definitely soured it for me," Mrs. Ross says. "There's something off about it."

One critic of the current youth soccer scene is Rick Meana, director of coaching for New Jersey Youth Soccer. Although Mr. Meana is also in charge of the state's Olympic Development Program for soccer—it's his job to identify the best young players statewide—he thinks that youth soccer has gotten way too competitive. He says he plans to address these concerns at Soccer Expo 2000, an event for parents and coaches scheduled for Jan. 8, 2000 at the New Jersey Convention and Exposition Center in Edison.

"There are parts of this country, and even this state, where we have kids that are 4 years old playing organized sports," Mr. Meana says. "That's too young."

As for traveling teams selected by a rigorous tryout process, he believes that should not start until about the age of 11.

To have 6- and 7-year-olds on traveling team is "absolutely ludicrous," he said. "You have kids learning that if they're not a winner, they're nothing. What we have forgotten to do is look at the child's development through various stages of growth."

Fred Engh, president of the National Alliance for Youth Sports who wrote *Why Johnny Hates Sports* (Avery Publishing Group), agrees that organized sports in this country start way too young.

"When we start the competitive sports with score boards, standings and championships, it's like putting *War and Peace* in front of a first-grader and saying, 'read,'" Mr. Engh said. "We're setting too many children up for failure."

Mr. Meana blames the current environment—he calls it "tournamentitis"—on the professionalization of youth soccer. "It's become a big business," he says. "There's a lot of money in youth soccer."

To be sure, parents have had a role in raising the stakes. After spending $250 to $400 a season to join a traveling soccer team, they want their children to win. That, in turn, puts pressure on coaches to develop a winning-first philosophy. Mr. Meana knows this firsthand, since he himself was a professional soccer coach in Delaware before taking his current position.

---

***"We have kids that are 4 years old playing organized sports. . . . That's too young."—***
**Rick Meana, director of coaching for New Jersey Youth Soccer.**

---

Then there is the time commitment to traveling soccer. Many teams practice twice a week and play once a weekend—often at distant matches. In programs like the one in Glen Ridge, the players are also required to play in the town's recreational league, which adds at least a fourth soccer outing to the week.

Even parents whose kids are thriving in travel soccer admit to soccer fatigue. "I didn't know what I was getting into," says Kathy Lesko, whose son Nicholas made the traveling team for 7 year olds in Glen Ridge. Among the things Ms. Lesko found she had to get used to was how often the schedules changed. She doesn't know for sure what time Nick will play on Sunday until the call comes Saturday night, meaning the family's weekend activities revolve around soccer.

"You adapt," said Mrs. Lesk. "We've missed a couple of birthday parties."

Jonathan Felsman of Maplewood—whose two sons, 9 and 10—was dismayed by the intensity of such programs, helped start an alternative league there three years ago. Like other parents, he felt that children might want more than the weekly game offered by the town's recreation program, but less than the full commitment of a traveling league.

"Our kids wanted a little more, and the only thing in town was a lot more," he recalls. "My big 'a hah' was when people were choosing synagogues." Many parents were turned off by religious school programs that required attendance three times a week. "I thought 'Why would you send them to soccer three days a week?'"

Mr. Felsman and his friends soon discovered a league nearby called the Intercounty Youth Soccer League, started by a father in Colonia in 1991 when his 11-year-old daughter was told she was too old to play in the town's recreational league.

The league started by the girl's father, Mike Burkert, soon began attracting players like his daughter, who had nowhere to play soccer, Mr. Burkert's league began to attract players who had "gotten burnt out by the age of 11 or 12" by the traveling leagues, he says.

Unlike traveling leagues, which select players and teams after several tryouts, registration in Intercounty is open to all—with the exception of high school varsity players and those on traveling teams. There are no "flights" or levels, and according to the mission statement, "it is recommended that talent within each town be distributed as evenly as possible." All players have to play at least half the game and no team is allowed to win by more than six goals. "You start to embarrass kids after six goals," Mr. Burkert said. "You start to hurt kids' feelings."

This is a relatively new concept to Mr. Hammond, who grew up playing soccer in Britain, where the sons of the ruling class take daily cold showers at Harrow and Eton.

"I grew up in a culture where if a team could beat you by 30, they would, and nobody cried about it," he said. But the pressure to prevent hurt feelings is pretty universal in America. If one of his teams is ahead by four goals, he said, "I slow down, move kids around, try to take my foot off the pedal. Some leagues have unwritten rules. They won't look kindly upon you" if your team wins by eight or nine goals.

But to Mr. Hammond, the thing that embarrasses kids the most are parents who are too involved. "They scream advice," he said. "They dissect performances. They tell them what they did wrong."

Not, however, if Mr. Hammond is nearby.

"My parents don't do this because they're totally trained," he said. "They're allowed to cheer—Well done! Hooray!—but nothing that might be a verb. No moving words. No coaching words."

Mr. Hammond admits, "Parents are very hard to deal with. That's the worst part of my job. I love them and I hate them."

# Out of Control[3]

BY WILLIAM NACK AND LESTER MUNSON
*SPORTS ILLUSTRATED,* JULY 24, 2000

It may have started as a simple skate-around at a nondescript hockey arena 15 miles north of Boston, with boys of all ages and sizes working on their puckhandling skills. But by the time it ended, amid children's wails over their dying father, it had become the final, ascendant symbol of a national malaise—of the violence and vulgarity that have been pooling like blood around youth sports in America. One hockey father, Michael Costin, lay slumped near the vending machines by the rink, his face so disfigured that two of his children would say they barely recognized him. Another hockey father, Thomas Junta, had thrown Costin to the ground and beaten him into a coma from which he would never awaken.

It all began around midafternoon on July 5, at the Burbank Ice Arena in Reading, Mass., when two men—Costin, 40, a part-time carpenter and a single father of four young kids, and Junta, 42, a truck driver and married father of two—got into what appeared to be a minor shoving match. Costin had been on the ice supervising the practice for the boys—who included his sons Brendan, 12, Michael, 11, and Sean, 10, and Junta's 10-year-old boy, Quinlan—when the action got a little rough. According to Junta's lawyer, Junta saw his son get checked and struck in the nose by an elbow. Junta complained, urging Costin to control the checking, but the attorney says that Costin skated over to where Junta was sitting and snapped, "That's what hockey is all about!"

When Costin came off the ice, Junta strode screaming toward him. The two men wrestled briefly—the 6'2", 275-pound Junta tore the 5'11", 175-pound Costin's shirt and ripped a gold chain from round his neck, according to Middlesex District prosecutors—until a rink employee broke up the scuffle and ordered Junta out of the arena. He left. In an era in which kids often behave with greater civility than their parents and in which violence and verbal abuse by adults have become commonplace at children's sporting events, the fight surprised no one in Reading, a town of some 23,000 souls. What happened next, however, shook a talk-show nation already numbed by pointless violence.

---

3. Reprinted courtesy of *Sports Illustrated* "Out of Control" by William Nack and Lester Munson, July 24, 2000. 

Costin and his boys were in the locker room, shedding their skates and gear, when young Michael said, "Dad, I'm thirsty." Moments later they were all at the Coke machine next to the rink when Junta returned, according to prosecutors, with "fists clenched." Junta knocked Costin down and pinned him to the floor with a knee on his chest. He then began beating Costin's face with his fists and banging his head on the hard rubber mats that covered the floor. Costin's three boys stood around Junta screaming, "Please stop! Please! He can't see. He can't hear." Junta did not stop, prosecutors say, until a bystander pulled him off. By the time police arrived, Costin lay unconscious, without a pulse, his head in a pool of blood, his face misshapen by the blows.

Junta was arrested on a charge of misdemeanor assault, but when Costin was pronounced dead two days later, prosecutors stiffened the charge to manslaughter—that is, killing Costin without meaning to. Junta has pleaded not guilty. His lawyer claims he struck Costin in self-defense and that he reentered the arena not to finish his fight with Costin but to look for two children he had driven to the rink. Junta is free on $5,000 bail, but he faces a trial after which, if found guilty, he could be sentenced to 20 years in prison.

Neither Junta nor Costin was new to the criminal justice system. Costin had been in prison seven times between 1983 and 1995 for crimes that stretched from breaking and entering to assaulting a cop, and Reading police believe he had ties to a gang of Hell's Angels in nearby Lynn, Mass. Junta had been charged with but found not guilty of willful destruction of property, had been sentenced to a year in jail for using a vehicle without the owner's permission and, in 1992, had been arrested for assault and battery. (There was no disposition in that case.)

Although the criminal records of the two men distinguish them from many Little League dads, the situation that triggered the violence is all too typical. Junta was regarded as a devoted father. Costin was a recovering alcoholic who had turned his life around after gaining custody of his four kids, and several acquaintances said he was "the consummate single father" who lived for his children. The kids—the three hockey-playing boys and their nine-year-old sister, Tara—trailed his casket as it was borne up the aisle of Our Lady of the Assumption Church in Costin's hometown of Lynnfield on July 11. The Reverend John E. Farrell delayed the funeral Mass to give the children time to finish writing letters of farewell to be placed in their father's casket. During the wake the grieving Tara had tried to climb into the coffin with her dad.

"Pride and anger can be virtuous and vicious," Farrell told the 200 mourners. "Sports can build up or take away."

As terrible and devastating as Costin's death was—in an ironic twist, Junta attacked Costin after Costin had rebuffed him for protesting violence in the practice—it was only the most recent case in what has become an epidemic of verbal harassment and physical violence by parents at youth sports events. Among the most egregious offenses:

- Ray Knight, the former Cincinnati Reds third baseman and manager, was charged with simple battery, disorderly conduct and affray (fighting in a public place) after an altercation at a girls' softball game in Albany, Ga., in April 1999. Knight engaged in a heated and profane 15-minute argument with the father of a girl on the team opposing the squad on which Knight's 12-year-old daughter was playing. Knight finally punched the man in the head.

***"Pride and anger can be virtuous and vicious. . . . Sports can build up or take away."*—Rev. John E. Farrell, Our Lady of the Assumption Church, Lynnfield, Mass.**

- Police had to be called to quell a brawl last October in which at least 50 parents and players went at one another at the end of a football game involving 11- to 13-year-olds in Swiftwater, Pa.
- After a hockey game for 11- and 12-year-old boys in Staten Island, N.Y., on Jan. 23, a carpenter named Matteo Picca struck his son's coach, Lou Aiani, in the face with two hockey sticks, according to witnesses, bloodying Aiani's nose. Picca, who was indicted for assault and criminal possession of a weapon and was sued for $4 million by Aiani, had been heard complaining angrily during the game that his son had not improved all season. Picca has pleaded not guilty to the charges and claims that while he did hit Aiani with his fist, he did not swing the sticks at the coach.
- Following a Little League game in Sacramento in April 1999, a man who was coaching his son's team beat up the manager of the opposing team. The assailant, who had been ejected by a 16-year-old umpire for verbally disrupting the game, was convicted of felony assault and sentenced to 180 days of work furlough.
- A Tamaqua, Pa., policeman was convicted of corruption of a minor and solicitation to commit simple assault for giving $2 to

a 10-year-old Little League pitcher to hit a batter with a fastball last August.

- A soccer dad in Eastlake, Ohio, pleaded no contest to a charge of assault last September after he punched a 14-year-old boy who had scuffled for the ball with the man's 14-year-old son, leading to both boys' ejections. The punch split the victim's lip. The man was sentenced to 10 days of community service and ordered to undergo counseling.
- A former corrections officer was sentenced to 30 days in jail for assaulting a 16-year-old ref in La Vista, Neb., last October at a flag football game for six- and seven-year-old boys.
- A youth baseball coach in Hollywood, Fla., was arrested for aggravated battery on July 12, almost a month after he broke an umpire's jaw with a punch during a Police Athletic League game for high school players. The umpire was throwing the coach out of the game when he was struck. The coach plans to plead not guilty.

The games kids play are looking more and more like dress rehearsals for the *Jerry Springer Show*. In fact, the fields and arenas of youth sports in North America have become places where a kind of psychosis has at times prevailed, with parents and coaches screaming and swearing at the kids, the officials or each other, and fights breaking out among adults. According to a survey conducted in the early 1990s by Michigan State University, of the 20 million American kids who participate in organized sports, starting as early as age four, about 14 million will quit before age 13, and they will say they dropped out mostly because adults—particularly their own parents—have turned the playing of games into a joyless, negative experience.

The vast majority of parents still comport themselves with restraint and civility at games, but it is impossible to ignore or wave away the loud, critical, ill-mannered parent in the stands who believes that his or her child is the next Junior Griffey or Mia Hamm. The obnoxious Little League parent, the meddling soccer mom, the aggressive dad who stalks the sidelines at football games and the poolside deck at swim meets have become a larger presence at youth games in the past five years. Fred Engh, president of the National Alliance for Youth Sports (NAYS), which educates coaches and parents on the needs of young athletes, says that field reports from his organization's 2,200 chapters in the U.S. reveal an alarming trend: In 1995 you could expect 5% of a crowd of parents to get out of line at a youth athletic event—i.e., to embarrass their children or be abusive toward the kids, officials and coaches. Only five years later, you can expect 15% of the crowd to cross the line. "It borders on insanity," says Engh. "Every year I see more and more ugly things."

Jim Thompson, director of the Positive Coaching Alliance at Stanford, says that 10 years ago, when he was giving coaching workshops, soccer parents and coaches (unlike their counterparts in baseball and basketball) had no complaints about parental behavior. But that was before soccer exploded in the U.S.—before it opened yet another lucrative mine of college scholarships and before the national women's team grew a comet's tail and rose in a spectacular arc to the world championship. Thompson says you should hear the lamentations now. Soccer folks talk about belligerent parents hurling abuse at officials. Indeed, says Thompson, things have become so difficult for youth-league soccer refs that adults are declining assignments, and the sport has had to turn to high schoolers for officiating. "But the kids don't want to do it either, because they don't want abuse from these parents," says Thompson.

***Adults . . . have turned the playing of games into a joyless, negative experience.***

The most serious problem facing the myriad organized youth sports leagues, however, involves a landmark case in which the Illinois Supreme Court is expected to decide later this year whether children's leagues can be held financially responsible for injuries resulting from adult violence at their games. The case grew out of a grotesque incident 10 years ago in which John Hills, the father-coach of a Little League player in the Chicago suburb of Lemont, complained to umpires that a rival coach, 16-year-old George Loy Jr. of suburban Bridgeview, was loudly making calls before the umpires themselves could make them. By the third inning Loy's father, George Sr., also a Bridgeview coach, was baiting Hills, calling him a "four-eyed mother—er" and promising to "get him after the game."

"After the sixth inning, as Hills bent over to pick up his scorebook, George Loy Sr. jumped him from behind, punching and kicking him as he drove him to the ground, and then circled the prostrate figure, looking for places to kick him again. George Jr. soon joined his father in pummeling Hills. Finally, George Sr.'s brother, Bridgeview manager Ted Loy, joined in the thuggery, kicking Hills between 10 and 15 times, witnesses said. Lemont's third-base coach, Harry Keeler, interceded and helped Hills to his feet and was hit himself. Then the Loys launched one last attack on Hills. George Sr. stepped in and dropped Hills with a right to the face that broke his nose, while George Jr. smashed Hills's left knee with an aluminum bat.

Hills did not wake up until he was in intensive care. Along with the broken nose, he suffered fractured ribs, a bruised kidney, a concussion, a scratched cornea and the injured knee, which still ails him. A plumber by trade, he returned to work only this year.

The Loy brothers were arrested, charged with battery and sentenced to supervision and 40 hours of community service. Hills sued all three Loys, the Bridgeview Little League Association and the Justice Willow Springs Little League, which sponsored the tournament and owned the field. After a two-week trial in which 19 witnesses described what had happened, a default judgment was entered against the Loys, who never responded to the service of legal papers. (Nor would they comment for this article.) A Chicago jury awarded Hills and his wife a total of $757,710, finding not only the Loys but also the two Little League associations liable for the damages. The Little League groups, whose insurance would pay their share of the award, appealed, but the three-judge Appellate Court in Chicago upheld the jury's judgment.

The outcome of the case created such anxiety at Little League's national headquarters in Williamsport, Pa., that the league hired a law firm to file an amicus curiae brief urging the seven Illinois Supreme Court justices to vacate the judgment. Little League has 2.7 million child-athletes and sponsors 186,000 teams in the U.S., and it sees a far-reaching danger if its local organizations are held accountable for the actions of parents and coaches. In a defense of its position, Little League declared that making its associations responsible for adult violence would put their playing fields in the same legal category as dens of potential mayhem like "taverns, discos and dance clubs." The brief notes that Little League games are alcohol-free events attended by children and their parents, and it asserts, "Little League baseball does not attract the less savory elements of the communities in which it thrives."

Remember that this brief grew out of an incident in which two men and a bat-wielding boy beat another man senseless while two teams of Little Leaguers stood and watched. If the Illinois Supreme Court sustains the jury verdict, thereby holding Little League's cleats to the fire, the whole topography of adult violence at children's games will change—just as court action altered the landscape on the issues of handguns and tobacco.

Outside the courtroom, as evidence of a national groundswell on the issue, various youth leagues and other groups have been at work to curb violence and encourage mature behavior at games. Over the last year and a half three U.S. government classes at Deer Valley High, outside Phoenix, initiated and nearly pushed through the Arizona legislature a bill called the Youth Sports Official Protection Act, which would stiffen penalties for violence against youth-league officials. The bill passed the state house of representatives 38-18 but was defeated 22-8 in the senate. The class will again lobby to pass the measure in the next school year.

Before the widely publicized class on sportsmanship held in February in Jupiter, Fla.—at which about 2,000 youth-league parents were required to sign a pledge to behave themselves at games—a soccer league outside Cleveland held a "Silent Sunday" last October in which parents were under league orders not to yell instructions to kids, not to question officials' calls and not even to let out a cheer. Many parents either sucked lollipops or put duct tape over their mouths.

West to east, meanwhile, youth-league violence kept police and lawyers working all last year and in the first half of this one. On April 27, 1999, in a slow-pitch softball game for 12-and-under girls in Albany, Ga., Ray Knight was coaching third base for the Magic, the team on which his daughter Erinn played. With the count 3-2 on a Magic batter, the pitcher for the opposing team, the Hot Dice, lofted a ball, and Knight, before the ump could make his call, loudly urged the batter to first: "Get on down there, atta baby!"

From behind the third-base dugout, a 47-year-old construction worker named Jimmy C. Smith, the father of a girl on the Hot Dice, yelled to Knight, "Let the umpire call the game!"

Knight turned around and said to Smith, "Are you talking to me?"

"Yeah, I'm talkin' to you!" Smith said.

Knight walked to the fence and said, "You don't tell me what to do!" He accused Smith of trying to embarrass him.

"You're doing a good enough job (of) embarrassing yourself," Smith said.

"You just shut up!" snapped Knight.

"You can't tell me to shut up!" Smith shouted back.

"Well, you just meet me here after the game," said Knight.

"I'll be here," said Smith.

After the game Knight saw Smith waiting off the field and walked over to him. They argued some more, and at one point Smith pushed Knight. Knight lost his temper, and soon both men were nose to nose and screaming obscenities at each other.

Just as the shouting ebbed and the fight seemed over, Smith started back toward the field. "You couldn't handle the big boys up there," he told Knight, referring to the major leagues, "so you had to come down here and coach girls' softball." As Smith walked by him Knight threw a punch that landed on Smith's right ear, opening a small cut. Smith dropped to one knee, and Dave Roberts, an assistant coach for the Hot Dice, grabbed Knight and took him to the ground to stop the fight. Knight did not resist.

It was all over by the time the cops arrived. The local district attorney, after interviewing witnesses, charged both Knight and Smith with two misdemeanors. Knight was also charged with simple battery for landing that punch. The charges are pending, and more than a year later Knight still regrets his loss of control. "I feel awful about it," he says. "I'll tell you how much it hurt me. My girls didn't play in that league this year. I didn't want any part of it. My remorse is immense."

Twelve days before Knight belted Smith, a more violent incident occurred at a Little League game involving seven- and eight-year-old boys and girls in south Sacramento. Lawrence Bahrs, the father and coach of a seven-year-old boy, became so disruptive that the 16-year-old umpire asked him to leave the field. Bahrs, a 40-year-old welder, was calling balls and strikes over the ump's voice. Bahrs says he had gotten angry at the other team's manager, James Solari, then 39, for allegedly instructing the umpire and for using abusive language. After the game, according to Sacramento Deputy District Attorney Scott Triplett, Bahrs lay in wait for Solari.

As Solari left the field, Bahrs recalls, he told Solari, "'You might think you're some kind of coach, but you're an a——.' That ticked him off, and he took a swing at me. I deflected it, and he backed away. I walked up to him and I decked him, and I punched him a couple of times and I kneed him in the face."

Solari says he suffered a concussion and had the braces on his teeth broken in the attack. Bahrs pleaded no contest to felony assault and served six months of work furlough. After his release, Bahrs attended court-ordered anger-management classes. He was also put on five years' probation. "I'm sorry it happened," Bahrs says, "but it's pretty prevalent. You think it's bad at baseball games, you ought to see it at soccer games."

Or midget football games. In Swiftwater, Pa., last Oct. 10, right after the Pocono Mountain Cardinals had defeated a team from Allentown's East Side Youth Center 14-7, the two teams of 11- to 13-year-old boys had met to shake hands when some of them began exchanging taunts. One angry lad shoved another, and Allentown's 13-year-old Nicholas Davis got whacked on the head by a helmet. Coaches tried to break it up, but the "footbrawl," as the Pocono Record would call it, ultimately involved 50 to 100 players and parents, most of whom were trying to break up the fight. A few of the parents joined the melee after they charged onto the field to rescue their kids. The police were summoned, but only three people were charged, one adult and two kids. Two people were injured; one, a Cardinals assistant coach, Michael Bartell, suffered a cut above his right eye that required seven stitches.

When asked in studies why they play sports, children invariably say they enjoy the fun, they like being with their friends, and they enjoy learning the fundamentals and improving their skills, according to Thomas Tutko, professor emeritus of sports psychology at San Jose State and a member of the NAYS board. "Kids rank winning about seventh or eighth down the list," says Tutko. Unlike pro and college sports, in which winning often translates into money, children's games are supposed to teach skills and values—such as fair play, working with others and dealing well with adversity—that kids can draw upon throughout their lives.

"The main purpose of youth sports is to emphasize effort, participation and skill development," says Joel Fish, director of the Center for Sports Psychology in Philadelphia. "So we are sending the wrong message when we get too invested in the outcome of a youth game—who won, who lost, who scored the most. You start to get away from what the mission of it is."

For more than 100 years, that mission has gone far beyond sport's chalk boundaries. In the 19th century, most immigrants to the U.S. came from industrializing countries in northern Europe, and they fit well into the newly industrializing America. After 1880, however, most immigrants were coming from small rural communities in southern and eastern Europe, where the agrarian economy did not prepare them for the regimentation of factory life. So across America, in schools, churches and playgrounds, games were organized both to get growing numbers of rowdy children off the streets and to teach the values of industrial production to recently arrived workers and their children.

"The organized playground movement and the emergence of organized sports were, in part, tied to the Americanization of workers," says Jay Coakley, a sports sociologist at the University of Colorado. "The playground movement was motivated strongly by the belief that you could use team sports to acculturate immigrants. You made them understand the notions of setting goals, of keeping records—the things that the assembly-line supervisor kept track of." After World War II, Coakley continues, games became instruments of organizing and controlling children as millions of urban Americans fled deteriorating cities, settled down behind white picket fences and bred like rabbits to produce the Baby Boom, perhaps the greatest population surge of any nation in Western history. "The average parents moved to suburbia to control their environment and to raise the kinds of children they wanted," says Coakley. "This led to the formation of supervised environments for kids."

Out of this singular set of circumstances emerged the vast, dust-choked world of youth sports. Armies of kids joined thousands of youth leagues, and their parents came out to watch them play. Indeed, the 1950s ushered in an epochal change in the nature of play in this country. For decades, unwatched and unfettered by adults, children had passed the time playing made-up street and schoolyard games—from stickball to kick-the-can—and in playing them had learned how to arbitrate their conflicts and needs, how to compromise, how to build a consensus and make their own rules. Which is to say, how to get along in a democratic society.

That era ended with the rise of youth sports organized and controlled by adults, who set up the leagues and the schedules, resolved

**"*We are sending the wrong message when we get too invested in the outcome of a youth game.*"—Joel Fish, Center for Sports Psychology, Philadelphia.**

disputes and made and enforced the rules. Children lost control of their games—along with all the skills they had learned by playing on their own—and the games themselves became extensions of the parents' lives, often more important to them than to the kids. So it was that a new species of bird was hatched in the aviary of U.S. sports: *Parentis vociferous*, the loud, intrusive moms and dads unable to restrain themselves.

The species has been sighted everywhere; it's native to all states, and anyone who has been involved in youth sports has a story to tell. Refs and umps are the easiest targets, particularly if they are young. Typical was the experience of Jesse Weber, 19, a sophomore microbiology major at Colorado who umpired Little League for five years in Shaw Heights, outside Denver, and who remembers the stream of catcalls from the stands. "It was ridiculous," Weber says. He remembers having to walk to the fence and tell adults twice as old as he, "You're out of line. Have some respect for the game and the players in it." He remembers parents who called him a "jackass" and followed him to the parking lot, as if to pick a fight. And he remembers the shame the children felt at their parents' behavior. "You could see it in their faces," Weber says.

Coaches and parents have been baiting youth-league umps for years. Robert Schwartz, executive director of the Juvenile Law Center in Philadelphia, was a 16-year-old umpire in a rec league for 10-year-olds when, after a championship game in 1966, he was followed by several parents as he walked, nearly in tears, the 100 yards from the field to the rec hall. "It was like 100 miles," Schwartz says. "They kept yelling, 'You're a piece of s——!' Nothing in my experience had prepared me to be called what I was called by those adults."

The umps aren't the only people in authority at youth sports who are upset by abusive parents. Melinda Schmitt was an All-America swimmer who took up coaching after graduating from Miami in 1980. "I loved to coach," she says. "Little kids to seniors." She was leading a team of eight-and-under children when she first saw how panting adults were ruining the experience for the kids, showing up with stopwatches and timing all the swimmers until they had to be barred from the pool deck.

At a meet in Pompano Beach, Fla., in 1982, one kid was finishing a 25-meter race when his father, dressed in a shirt and slacks, left the stands and leaped into the waist-deep pool. He started slapping the water right next to the child. "He was screaming in the kid's face, 'You didn't finish hard enough! You let them pass you!'" Schmitt recalls. That incident, more than anything else, drove her out of coaching. "I still think about going back," she says. "But I don't want to deal with the parents. They're trying to live out their fantasies. Some of them think they have the next Mark Spitz."

> ***A new species of bird was hatched in the aviary of U.S. sports:* Parentis vociferous, *the loud, intrusive moms and dads unable to restrain themselves.***

One of the distinguishing marks of obnoxious sports parents, psychologists say, is the inflated hopes they have for their children—an implacable belief, unsupported by evidence, that their kids are Mozarts in cleats, gifted enough to earn a college scholarship or even be a professional. With all the elite club and travel teams now playing, children's games have grown as deadly serious as intercollegiate sports. Not incidentally, the rise of *Parentis vociferous* coincided with the transformation of sports into a secular religion—and the escalating value of college scholarships and pro contracts.

"Like pro sports, youth sports at many levels are no longer a game," says Darrell J. Burnett, a clinical child psychologist in Laguna Niguel, Calif., who specializes in youth sports. "It is big business. The statistical chances of a kid getting a college scholarship are very small, but parents have unreasonable expectations.

When their kid makes an error at shortstop, instead of saying, O.K., he made a mistake, he'll learn from it, they think, Oh, my god! What if a scout is in the stands watching?"

Now Armageddon can be found in tee-ball games for five-year-olds, and battles have been joined in events as trivial as flag-football games for six- and seven-year-old boys in which no official score is kept. Last Oct. 23, in La Vista, Neb., a 38-year-old machinist and former corrections officer, Roenee Ware, was caught on videotape verbally abusing and then assaulting the 16-year-old referee, Mike Tangeman, at halftime of a game. Flag football is a weighty business in Nebraska. Ware's team of tykes, the La Vista Tornadoes, had three coaches—Ware was the offensive coordinator—and the Tornadoes were "running the option," says Tangeman. When the game got rough and elbows started to fly, the ref began calling penalties. At halftime, Ware went onto the field and yelled at him for his calls.

The tape shows Ware, 6'3" and 250 pounds, jabbing his finger in Tangeman's chest as the little boys, including Ware's son, gathered behind him. At one point, after a shoving match, the 5'9", 160-pound ref slapped Ware's finger away. Ware then punched him in the face. Ware was arrested on a charge of third-degree assault and convicted at trial. He was contrite at his April 14 sentencing—"I should have walked away," he said—but Sarpy County Judge Todd Hutton gave him 30 days in jail and fined him $585.

Among the central questions raised by such a litany of incidents, says Jim Thompson of the Positive Coaching Alliance, is this: "Why do parents and coaches in youth sports act in a way they would never act in other places?"

"Everything starts at the pro level and funnels down to the college and the youth sports level," says Leonard Zaichkowsky, head of the sports psychology program at Boston University. "At Fenway Park, people with multicolored hair strip off their shirts to show tattoos and body paint, and a certain kind of clientele prides itself on drinking and using foul language."

What makes a youth-league event even more emotionally charged is that parents are watching their own children play, their own DNA body paint and tattoos, and everyone knows that blood is thicker and more volatile than beer. "Something deep down inside happens in moms and dads when they see their kid up there with the bases loaded," says Joel Fish. "These are well-intentioned parents. We know the people booing the loudest are pretty straitlaced in their everyday lives. I can't tell you how many times I've heard a parent say: 'Did I really yell at the 16-year-old umpire? Did I really yell at my kid?'"

Last Sept. 25, at a high school soccer game in Eastlake, Ohio, George Telidis, a 40-year-old Greek immigrant and former scholarship soccer player at Cleveland State, went racing onto the field after, he says, he saw his 14-year-old son, Alex, go down twice while fighting for the ball with a 14-year-old Bosnian immigrant, Davor Jozic. Alex has braces, and Telidis says he saw his son's mouth bleeding. "You kind of lose it when you see your own son's blood," Telidis says. He belted Jozic in the mouth, splitting the boy's lip. (A teacher of Jozic's says both boys had been red-carded for the incident and were walking off the field when Telidis struck.) Telidis was arrested for assault, to which he pleaded no contest, and was sentenced to 10 days of community service. He seems chagrined now. "I would not hit him if I could do it over," Telidis says. "I would control myself more. I did what I did to defend my son."

The whole parenting experience is emotionally loaded, says child sports psychology consultant Alan Goldberg, and in sports it often stirs feelings that have been buried for years. "All the old garbage comes to the surface," Goldberg says. "If *you* were frustrated as an athlete, if *you* were never picked to play on a team or didn't go anywhere as an athlete, all that stuff gets tapped into."

Frank Smoll, a sports psychologist at Washington who specializes in youths in sports, speaks of a "reverse dependency trap" between young athletes and their parents. Normally, Smoll says, youngsters depend upon their parents for feelings of self-worth and self-esteem. The trap is set when the parent overidentifies with the child. "So it's not just Johnny or Mary out there," Smoll says. "The *parents* are playing the game out there, maybe trying to live out a past glory or attain some athletic excellence they were denied or incapable of attaining."

Over one 12-year period, Burnett says, he worked with as many as 1,000 troubled youths in Southern California. "Runaways, drug users, suicidal kids," Burnett says. "Ninety-eight percent of these kids had dropped out of youth sports. I asked them why. Kid after kid gave the same two reasons: negative coaches and negative parents." Burnett and other psychologists recall the common plea of children to their parents: "Please don't yell on the sideline. It's distracting. And it's so embarrassing."

In Goldberg's archive of horrors, the pièce de résistance is the memory of an irate mother at poolside during a swim meet, slapping her nine-year-old daughter across the face in front of everyone and screaming, "Don't you ever do that to me again!" The girl had shown up late for her heat and been disqualified. "Know why she missed the race?" Goldberg says. "Her mother never asked. She missed her race because two heats earlier her best friend had had a lousy swim and was devastated and sobbing in the locker room. This girl had been in there comforting her."

# Second Impact Syndrome: Sports Confront Consequences of Concussions[4]

BY JEFFREY H. TYLER AND MICHAEL E. NELSON
*USA TODAY,* MAY 2000

Each year, more than 300,000 people suffer brain injuries while playing a sport, most of which are concussions. In football slang, players say a team member got "dinged" or had his "bell rung." Boxers who get stunned by a blow to the head may be described as "punch-drunk." What an athlete experiences during a concussion is actually a temporary, trauma-induced alteration in mental status. Many concussions occur without the individual ever losing consciousness, but researchers have determined that even a seemingly minor "bell-ringing" in the course of play can cause lasting physical and mental injury, or even result in death.

Sports concussions have become more publicized recently, as celebrity athletes announce early retirement, and tragic accidents and major lawsuits in sports are covered more closely by the media. Nevertheless, such injuries persist across the country in recreational and school sports where clear preventive guidelines for managing head injuries are slow to reach the field.

Studies released by the American Academy of Neurology and the National Brain Injury Association indicate that 10% of college and 20% of high school football players receive brain injuries in any given season. Most of these are transitory, but those who suffer a first concussion may be four times more likely to suffer a second than someone who has never had one.

Researchers have identified a serious series of brain injury events they call second impact syndrome (SIS). According to James P. Kelly, director of the Brain Injury Program at the Rehabilitation Institute of Chicago, SIS occurs when an athlete suffers a mild head injury, returns to play too soon, and suffers what may be a relatively minor second hit before the brain has fully healed. If the second injury occurs while the individual still has symptoms from the first impact, the result can be a rapid, catastrophic increase in pressure

4. Article by Jeffrey H. Tyler and Michael E. Nelson from *USA Today* May 2000. 

within the brain. Effects of SIS include physical paralysis, mental disabilities, and epilepsy. Death can occur approximately 50% of the time.

"SIS can affect anyone exposed to a mild or moderate concussion; there's no age discrimination," notes Kelly. "But it seems to affect teenagers more often because they are the least likely to report their injuries or take the time to recover from a concussion when they do get hurt. They head back into the game too soon, not fully aware of the risks they are taking."

It is unclear how many cases of SIS occur each year in the U.S. because the first injury is not usually reported to a physician. The Center for Disease Control counted 17 cases of SIS between 1992 and 1995, but experts believe that the true numbers are higher. Most cases involve male adolescents or young adults, who received a second catastrophic concussion while participating in football, boxing, ice hockey, or snow skiing.

The case of Brandon Schultz, a high school football player from Anacortes, Wash., is a prime example of the devastating consequences of SIS. Schultz's recently resolved lawsuit against the Anacortes School District is the first of its kind to argue that a school district was negligent for failing to prevent an SIS injury.

On Oct. 25, 1993, just two weeks after his 16th birthday, Schultz's life changed forever when he made a tackle during the final seconds of the first half of a junior varsity football game. Viewed from the field, and by his parents' home video recording, the tackle looked harmless enough. It did not appear that Schultz made head-to-head contact with another player, let alone received a concussion.

Schultz was slow to get up, but did not appear to lose consciousness. After a minute or two, he stood and returned to the end zone for the halftime huddle. Schultz was able to walk and talk, telling his coach only that his head hurt. Ten minutes later, he collapsed into a fit of seizures before losing consciousness, the result of uncontrollable brain swelling. During this 10-minute period, Schultz's brain essentially exploded inside his skull.

What his parents' game tape did not show is that, one week earlier, Schultz was pulled from play following a concussion that left him momentarily unconscious. He had suffered headaches throughout the week and was held out of practice, but was never referred to a doctor by his coaches.

Schultz is now confined to a neurological facility in California and still suffers daily from the consequences of his injury. His physicians have described his condition as being locked in a state of permanent adolescence. His cognitive functions are impaired, and he requires almost constant supervision because of his ongoing behavioral difficulties. As a result of the many strokes suffered in the aftermath of his injury, Schultz also experiences motor control problems on his left side and must wear a brace to walk.

Seattle attorney Michael E. Nelson [one of this article's authors], himself a survivor of a serious brain injury, was able to negotiate a pre-trial settlement of Schultz's lawsuit. Nelson's legal argument was that the school district was liable for negligence when it failed to require Schultz to see a doctor after his first concussion. The school district's coaches regularly required a medical clearance following even minor orthopedic injuries, but did not do so in the case of Schultz's initial concussion.

The confidential settlement amount should provide the lifetime care required for Schultz. Experts have estimated that his lifetime

***"[Teenagers] . . . are the least likely to report their injuries or take the time to recover from a concussion when they do get hurt."*— James P. Kelly, director of the Brain Injury Program, Rehabilitation Institute of Chicago.**

care costs will exceed $12,000,000.

Many athletes and their parents do not grasp the risk of returning to sports while still suffering even mild concussion symptoms. Most concussions occur without a loss of consciousness, so players and their parents may not realize that a persistent headache indicates that the athlete's brain has not yet recovered from the first blow. The American Academy of Neurology and the National Brain Injury Association have issued recommendations for return to play. The guidelines divide concussions into three types:

**Grade I:** No loss of consciousness; transient confusion; mental status abnormalities last less than 15 minutes. The athlete may play again that day if symptoms resolve within 15 minutes.

**Grade II:** No loss of consciousness; transient confusion; mental status abnormalities last more than 15 minutes. The athlete can play again only after he or she has been symptom-free for a full week.

**Grade III:** Any loss of consciousness, either for brief seconds or prolonged. An athlete who is unconscious for just a few seconds can resume play after a full week of no symptoms. If the loss of consciousness lasts several minutes or more, the waiting period is at least two weeks.

Researchers from the Henry Ford Health Systems, Detroit, Mich., have been working with the National Football League, National Hockey League, and National Collegiate Athletic Association to promote a new, more-individualized system to determine when an athlete who has suffered a concussion can safely return to competition. Currently, most physicians rely on various grading systems that rank symptoms and recommend varying lengths of symptom-free observation—ranging from 20 minutes to several weeks—before allowing an athlete to return to play.

According to Mark R. Lovell, head of the Ford Division of Neuropsychology, those guidelines no longer reflect the state of medical knowledge. "For years, our understanding of concussion has been modeled after boxing," thus placing the greatest weight on loss of consciousness. However, physicians have learned that "short-circuiting," which occurs when brain tissue slams against the inside of the skull, can often make itself known in a more gradual way. "We see players who weren't even close to being knocked out who later develop symptoms that suggest more severe concussions, and players who are knocked out who afterward have very little in the way of symptoms." The best way to tell if an athlete's mental processes have returned to normal, he argues, is to compare them with data from preseason tests of memory skills and reaction times.

Stephen Rice, a national expert on pediatric sports medicine at the Jersey Shore Medical Center in Neptune, N.J., argues that the best tool for preventing catastrophic brain injuries is seeing a doctor. In reviewing SIS incidents, he discovered there has never been a documented case of SIS when the injured player was referred to a physician after the first impact. According to Rice and other head injury experts, the referral of the concussion victim to a physician after first impact is an effective preventive measure.

To minimize future SIS tragedies, Nelson is pushing for standard head injury instructions for parents to use when their child suffers any sort of head injury. Nelson is also urging school districts to have sports officials use similar brain injury prevention guidelines and develop better health education programs for athletes and coaches.

"When a school district operates a sports program, it has the obligation to operate a safe program," says Rice. "Conversely, if a school district cannot operate a safe sports program, should it have the right to run a sports program at all?"

**Pro Athletes Feel the Blow**

Concussion risks do not end with teenage athletes. In professional sports, participants can suffer the cumulative effect of repeated concussions, otherwise known as post-concussion syndrome (PCS). With each successive blow, the damaged brain takes longer to heal or never recovers to the pre-trauma state, so that each injury becomes more severe. As with SIS, players are much more likely to become impaired from a second injury following a previous concussion.

Veteran New York Ranger defenseman Jeff Beukeboom announced his retirement from hockey in July 1999, after suffering three concussions in his last season. Beukeboom was the second Rangers player to retire in two years due to post-concussion syndrome, exiting on the heels of center Pat LaFontaine.

Beukeboom claims he suffered 5 to 10 concussions during his 13-year career. Since his last injury in February, 1999, he continues to experience headaches and loss of concentration in conversations. With a family that includes three small children, Beukeboom says that everyday tasks have become a chore and that his memory is spotty. He can no longer concentrate enough to train physically.

Multiple concussions, even when spaced several months or years apart, can have serious neurological consequences. Behavioral and magnetic resonance tests have proven that repeated concussions result in decreased mental performance, brain atrophy, and dementia. These physical features, normally associated with Parkinson's disease, were noted in boxers and termed Dementia Pugilistica.

Currently, the NHL and NFL are taking steps to understand and manage sports concussions better. An NHL official who would not comment on Beukeboom's retirement did maintain the league is at the forefront of all major sports by conducting mandatory baseline screening at training camp.

One clinical researcher agrees. "The NHL set a precedent, a truly great example for the rest of the professional sports industry to emulate," maintains Rosemarie Scolaro Moser, director of the RSM Psychology Center in Lawrenceville, N.J. "They provide a strong and comprehensive model that educational institutions should also be judged by. The baseline screening may be the one tool we can use accurately to keep players from returning to their sport too soon. If we can keep them safe from a critical SIS injury or PCS, we can potentially prevent concussions and more serious brain damage."

Sensitive to the invisible symptoms of concussions, the NHL is taking precautions to help prevent them. LaFontaine and Philadelphia Flyers center Eric Lindros, whose brother Brett was forced to retire from the New York Islanders following repeated concussions, contributed to the development of shock-absorbing mouth guards and more-protective helmet designs to reduce susceptibility to concussions. Today, more players are voluntarily wearing mouth guards to decrease their risks. (Meanwhile, Eric Lindros' career is threatened by a series of concussions.)

In addition, the league's Board of Governors in 1999 ordered that all NHL arenas using seamless glass technology be fitted with a board system called CheckFlex, which provides more "give" on contact and could reduce concussions. Despite this step, some rinks still have not installed it.

***Sensitive to the invisible symptoms of concussions, the NHL is taking precautions to help prevent them.***

The NFL has also lost its share of players to multiple concussions and is reacting. NFL Charities has funded a program at Thomas Jefferson University Hospital in Philadelphia to study Philadelphia Eagles players who sustain concussions during game actions. Researchers hope to examine eight players during the next two years.

"Ultimately, we want to use data from our study to construct a clinical examination that can be used right when a player comes to the sideline with a concussion during an actual game," indicates John McShane, team physician for the Eagles and director of primary care sports medicine at the hospital.

As part of the study, when someone sustains a concussion, he will first undergo magnetic resonance spectroscopy, which looks at brain metabolism and detects chemical markers that trace physical changes in the brain. Next, researchers will test coordination, reasoning, and concentration skills. The players will continue to undergo exams until the results return to normal. By correlating test results, researchers can determine when the ill effects of a concussion have disappeared.

The key to reducing an athlete's risk is for players, coaches, trainers, and parents to know the symptoms of concussion and how to manage them. The pro leagues have immense resources and team physicians to assess the symptoms on the sidelines. Many suburban high schools keep certified athletic trainers on site for games, and a number have doctors on the sidelines. Yet, a safety gap remains in many school systems and recreational leagues, where only a coach and players may be on hand during practices and games.

The American Academy of Neurology and the National Brain Injury Association offer the following guidelines for operating a high school or youth sports program focused on safe, proper brain injury management:

- Adequate education for coaches, including sufficient knowledge of head injuries and symptom management.

- Clearly defined standards regarding when and why to refer athletes to physicians.
- A comprehensive system for athletic health care, including these elements: a team physician; athletic trainers; formal education in sports medicine for coaches; informed consent by parents and athletes regarding risks of head injuries; head injury information sheets for parents; requiring that a player with a head injury visit a doctor and receive a return-to-play note; and developing clearly defined and appropriate criteria for returning to play after head injuries.

As the result of the Brandon Schultz lawsuit, the Anacortes School District has donated funds for his mother, Lane Phelan, to travel to school districts and brain injury organizations nationwide to educate parents and players about the dangers of concussion in sports. "I want parents and players to know that concussions are always serious—every concussion has the potential for a catastrophic outcome," she says. "When there are any signs of a concussion, whether it's just a headache or nausea, you need to seek medical attention."

# III. College and Semi-Pro Sports

*Quarterback Josh Heupel of the University of Oklahoma Sooners celebrates the team's National Championship at the Orange Bowl on January 3, 2001. The Sooners beat the Seminoles of Florida State University, 13-2.*

# *Editor's Introduction*

Many boys and girls who grow up playing organized sports dream of making it into the "big leagues" some day. They see their favorite professional athletes performing amazing feats and want to know the thrill of accomplishing marvels while being adored by—and earning—millions. For most young players, the primary means of reaching this goal is through attending college, usually on an athletic scholarship. Others forgo a college education to play for minor league teams, earning small but decent salaries while waiting to be called up to "the show" by big league franchises. The experiences of these aspiring athletes is the subject of Section III, which considers college and semi-professional sports.

David Meggyesy, whose article "Athletes in Big-Time College Sport" begins the section, explores the sometimes impossible expectations and pressures put on college athletes—especially in NCAA Division I colleges and universities—to maintain their grades while bringing their school a national championship. He also examines the racism that exists in college sports and the manner in which minority athletes are exploited by their schools. Until the 1970s, college sports were also plagued by sexism, but that situation was amended by the passage of Title IX, which prohibits colleges and universities from giving preference to men when distributing athletic scholarships. The result has been a marked increase in women's sports programs and the number of female athletes on college campuses. Nevertheless, as Andrew Zimbalist explains in "Backlash Against Title IX: An End Run around Female Athletes," many are now seeking to restrict once again the number of athletic scholarships given to women, claiming that male sports programs and male athletes have been neglected recently in the attempt to compensate for years of sexist policies.

While colleges and universities reap the benefits of their teams' success, gaining in national prestige and earning millions in TV revenue dollars, the student athletes earn nothing and cannot profit from their own achievements. Many believe this situation is extremely unfair, as Craig T. Greenlee demonstrates in his article "College Athletes Deserve Some Equity." Greenlee explains how NCAA regulations that prohibit the students' acceptance of gifts from school backers often place what he considers unjust restrictions on naive students, many of whom come from financially disadvantaged backgrounds. Greenlee foresees a time when this system will be reformed, thereby enabling college athletes to share in the profits they generate for their schools.

For those young athletes with little interest in college who would still like to earn their living in professional sports, minor league organizations—including baseball, hockey, and basketball—provide an alternate route to the big leagues. An article for *Sports Illustrated*, "Inside the NBA: Springing a League," reports on the formation of one such organization, which may soon become affiliated with the NBA. Franchise owners have high hopes for its success, given the fact that, with ticket prices for professional sporting events rising each year, minor league sports have gained in popularity during the 1990s. Matthew J. Brenthal and Peter J. Graham look at this development from a marketing perspective in "Base Hits: There Are Major-league Benefits in the Minors." The writers examine how factors like low ticket prices and high entertainment value make minor league games appealing to spectators.

# Athletes in Big-Time College Sport[1]

By Dave Meggyesy
*Society*, March/April 2000

> *We are living in a time when college athletics are honeycombed with falsehood, and when the professions of amateurism are usually hypocrisy. No college team ever meets another with actual faith in the other's eligibility.*
>
> —President William Funce of Brown University, in a speech before the National Education Association, 1904.

In responding to Professor Harry Edward's essay regarding black athletes in "amateur" college sport, my focus will be on the National Collegiate Athletic Association's (NCAA) 114 Division IA colleges and universities, particularly the top 50 or so "power schools" and their revenue producing football and basketball sports programs. At these institutions we see the most glaring contradictions between the avowed educational mission of these schools' athletic programs, their governing organization (the NCAA) and the commercial reality of their athletic departments and the NCAA itself. Athletic departments at these top athletic schools are highly profitable sports entertainment enterprises.

Overseeing virtually all post-secondary sports programs in the United States, the NCAA was founded in 1905 in response to the rising death toll in college football and increasing "professionalism" of college sports in general. Its mission, then and now, is "to maintain intercollegiate athletics as an integral part of the educational program and the athlete as an integral part of the student body." College sports programs, then and now, are conceived as amateur educational experiences that benefit and enhance the overall education of students who happen to be athletes.

As a non-profit educational association, the NCAA administers college sport and promulgates and enforces rules agreed upon by its 1,027 member schools that provide athletic programs for approximately 325,000 athletes. The NCAA, with an annual budget of $32 million, employs approximately 270 people.

The NCAA member schools are divided into three divisions (I, II, III) based on school size. Division I is further divided into three Divisions (IA, IAA, IAAA) based primarily on a school's athletic

1. Article by David Meggyesy from *Society* March/April 2000. Copyright © *Society*. Reprinted with permission.

department's ability to generate revenue, stadium seating capacity and student body size. In its present form, the NCAA is dominated by the approximately fifty Division IA "power schools" whose athletic departments field the top college football and men's basketball teams and are profit centers for their universities based on their highly successful sports programs. Women's basketball at some of

***Make no mistake, big-time college football and basketball programs are now . . . a multi-billion dollar sports entertainment enterprise.***

these top schools, the University of Tennessee and Stanford University for example, run programs that are highly successful and profitable. At these top athletic schools, football and basketball revenues fund the overall athletic department and its non-revenue producing sports programs and still show a profit.

An 18-member executive committee governs the NCAA. Although the 318 Division I schools comprise 31% of the NCAA membership, they hold 13 (or 72%) of the seats on the executive committee. Within the governance structure of Division I, of the 15-member board of directors, nine members (or 60%) come from Division IA schools. In addition, Division IA schools hold 18 seats on the 34-member Division I Management Council.

In commercial terms, during the last 20 years, revenue-producing college sport has exploded. NCAA member school sports revenues have increased 8000% since 1976 and NCAA revenues went from $6.6 million in 1977–78 to $267 million in 1997–98. Make no mistake, big-time college football and basketball programs are now, collectively, a multi-billion dollar sports entertainment enterprise.

**Education versus Commerce**

The primary contradiction within the NCAA and, in particular, its top revenue producing schools is that, on one hand the amateur rules apply to the athletes and on the other, the rules of the market apply to the school's athletic departments with the big exception being their labor costs. Putting it a different way, on one hand the NCAA and its member schools are non-profit educational entities, with their athlete employees categorized as student athletes, and on the other their athletic departments, at the top level, are highly profitable commercial enterprises. Interestingly, various federal courts have recognized college athletic departments, as competing commercial entities whose activities fall within the purview of federal anti-trust laws.

In a recent case, in March 1999, the NCAA reached a $54.5 million settlement with entry-level college coaches who had sued the NCAA on anti-trust grounds. In 1991 the NCAA Division I schools by a nearly unanimous vote agreed to cap entry-level coach's salaries at $12,000 per year and $4,000 for the summer. The coaches sued and in 1995 a federal court found the NCAA violated anti-trust law. The NCAA appealed the case to the U.S. Supreme Court where its petition was denied, thus opening the door for the settlement.

As athletic departments at our major universities have explicitly become sports entertainment businesses, the athletes, unfortunately, still must function under the original NCAA mandate as "amateur student-athletes" who don't get paid for their athletic labor. By continuing to define, what are essentially athlete employees as "amateur student-athletes," the *college athlete labor market* does not fall under federal or state antitrust laws or state workers compensation laws. As such, any compensation or lack thereof that athletes receive, which the NCAA member schools as economic competitors have conspired to and agreed upon, cannot be challenged in anti-trust court. Further, by defining athlete employees as amateur student-athletes, workers compensation benefits due to injury on the job are non-existent. In this existing relationship between the athletes, who, in the final analysis, produce the revenues, and the schools, who present the games and reap the financial windfall, lies the fertile field of exploitation of human labor and an underground or black-market economy that trades in young, primarily black athletes.

### Athletic Scholarship System

Central to the athletic scholarship system is an implied quid pro quo; student athletes will receive a quality college education in trade for four years of athletic service. However, there is a significant flaw in the economic argument that justifies not paying a revenue-producing athlete cash money because of his or her athletic scholarship cost. Adding 100 scholarship student athletes to a 10,000 undergraduate student body minimally increases the overall costs of educating the total, in this example, the 10,100 undergraduate student body. The university's absorbing the scholarship cost for 100 student athlete's athletic scholarships is really a "paper expense," because the actual *education cost* for scholarship athletes is absorbed by the university's undergraduate program. No extra capital expenditures are necessary to accommodate the additional 100 student-athletes, nor is the school required to hire extra professors to teach them. For sure, expenses for room and board are real costs, yet compared to revenues generated, they are miniscule. With this essentially cost-free labor pool, it is small wonder big-time programs are so profitable.

In the present system the most important issue for black and white scholarship student athletes alike is whether or not they will receive a legitimate college education and degree that is translatable to meaningful and financially viable work as "payment" for their athletic services. Unfortunately, in most cases they will not. Looking at graduation rates for incoming National Football League

---

***Student athletes' participation in college revenue producing sports programs . . . continues to reveal a century-long pattern of exploitation of student athletes.***

---

(NFL) players, of the 211 rookies on NFL teams in 1998 only 13, or 6 percent, had graduated. In August 1999 *The Chronicle of Higher Education* reported: "Graduation rates of football players and of men's and women's basketball players at colleges in the NCAA's top division have fallen to their lowest levels in seven years. The report also states, "the new figures show fewer black athletes graduating than at any time since the mid-1980s" when Proposition 48 was instituted to help solve the problem. In the Division I revenue producing sports, football and men's basketball, 51% of football players graduated and 41% of male basketball players graduated after six years. According to the report, only 33% of Division I black male basketball players graduated in six years, the lowest graduation rate since 1985.

*The Chronicle* . . . does not examine the quality of education measured in part by the potential future "worth" of a particular degree. Clearly a degree in engineering or a quality liberal arts degree will be potentially worth more than a degree in criminal justice or recreation. Examining kinds of degrees earned by NFL players shows a preponderance of athlete graduates fall into what could be called the non-academic degree category athletes. This pattern is not so much an affirmation of the "dumb jock" stereotype but rather is a product of an athletic/academic structure that severely limits educational opportunity for scholarship athletes. Participation in a top revenue-producing program is more than a full-time job as numerous commentators have pointed out with extended seasons, away game travel, off-season conditioning and strength-training programs and in-season practice and meetings.

### The Black Athlete

Student athletes' participation in college revenue producing sports programs, which are dominated by black athletes, continues to reveal a century-long pattern of exploitation of student athletes. As black athletes increasingly dominate college revenue producing sports the burden of this exploitive system falls on their shoulders. The plight of the black athlete, in what could by understatement be called a system of athletic exploitation, is a matter of degree compared to white athletes. However it is more severe due to an underlying pattern and consequence of racism in college sports as well as the larger society. Nevertheless, the most onerous issues black athletes face in Division IA revenue producing sports programs, primarily football and basketball, are almost identical to those faced by white athletes. By way of analogy, when Jerry Kramer the white All-Pro Green Bay Packer guard who played for the late legendary NFL coach, Vince Lombardi, was asked if Lombardi treated black football players differently than whites, his reply was, "Not really, he treats us all like dogs."

For the black athlete there still exist a number of other issues revolving around race that exacerbates their plight in our country's top college athletic programs. For example, the virtual lack of black coaches and athletic directors in Division IA programs and remnants of racially motivated "stacking," the practices of denying black athletes access to certain positions on a football team. Historically, in big-time college and professional football, blacks had been denied access to what were called the "thinking" positions, "the lilly white triangle," the center, two guards and quarterback for example. Black football players were "stacked" in positions thought to merely require raw talent and athleticism, running back and defensive back, for example.

However, due to increasing economic pressure during the last decade on coaching staffs in the top programs to "win and win now," and changing social attitudes, black athletes now star in all college football team positions including quarterback. Given the chance, black athletes are becoming the best players at these former "white" positions exemplified by the fact that three black and two white college quarterbacks were number one picks in the 1999 NFL college player draft.

While the NCAA and its Division IA member schools exploit the talents of black athletes and deny these same athletes access to a quality education, they also limit employment opportunities to blacks athletes after their athletic career ends. For the 1999 season in the 114 Division IA college football programs, black players comprised 51% of the total while there were only five black head coaches equaling 4% of the total. Black Division I basketball coaches comprised 28%, 86 out of 310. Clearly, for black athletes, opportunities for career advancement in their sport beyond their athletic career are virtually non-existent. A glass ceiling is a fact of life for black coaches and athletic administrators in "big-time" college sports programs as it is, incidentally, in the NFL, National Basketball Association (NBA) and Major League Baseball.

Shoring up this fiction of the amateur student-athlete, and, in an attempt to blunt rising criticism of this exploitive system, the NCAA member schools in 1983 enacted Proposition 48. Ten years before in 1973, in response to a rising tide of student athlete protests, primarily by black athletes, the NCAA Division IA schools eliminated their four-year athletic grants-in-aid (athletic scholarships) converting them to one-year renewable grants. With the one-year renewable scholarship the head coach and athletic department had a bigger hammer to control the athletes. If an athlete misbehaves in the eyes of the coach, his scholarship can be terminated. Critics pointed out that Prop. 48 was a not so veiled attempt to reduce the number of black scholarship athletes, assuming that more high school black athletes than whites would be unable to meet the Proposition 48 requirements. In fact this assumption has turned out to be the case. As Dr. Edwards's article points out, "In the first two years of Proposition 48 enforcement 92% of all academically ineligible basketball players and 84% of academically ineligible football players were black athletes."

Proposition 48, as an attempt to legitimize the educational mission of the Division I revenue producing college sports programs by establishing minimal academic standards for incoming student athletes, had the unspoken and, some would say, desired effect on black athletes. It was devastating. However Proposition 48 also caused an unintended effect; not only did it negatively impact black athletes as a group, it potentially eliminated superior black athletes who were coveted by the top athletic programs. In response, the NCAA in 1990 instituted Proposition 42 to "loophole" Proposition 48 creating a category of potential scholarship athlete called "partial qualifiers." However, as Dr. Edwards points out, the net effect of both propositions 48 and 42 ". . . has been to limit the opportunities—both educational and athletic—that would otherwise be available to black youth."

In 1996, as an amendment to Proposition 48, the NCAA adopted Proposition 16 which established a minimum 820 score on the Scholarship Aptitude Test (SAT) for incoming scholarship athletes, over protests from minority groups including the Black Coaches Association. In March 1999, federal Judge Ronald Buckwalter in *Cureton v. NCAA* ruled the NCAA could not use minimum test scores to eliminate student athletes from eligibility because the practice is discriminatory and unfair to blacks. On December 22, 1999, in a two-to-one decision, the U.S. Third Circuit Court of Appeals reversed Judge Buckwalter's ruling on a technicality. The Appellate Court did not address the primary issue in the case.

Judge Buckwalter's ruling, I believe, signaled a fresh assessment of the NCAA mission and the role of revenue producing sports programs at our major universities, particularly now, given the significant revenues involved. At the heart of his ruling is the issue of discrimination and exploitation, particularly of black athletes that is embedded in, an almost century-old system of athlete exploitation in collegiate revenue producing sports. Furthermore, Judge Buckwalter's decision points directly to a fundamental issue the NCAA has been dancing around for years, which is equitable compensation in real dollars for athletes who generate these enormous college sports revenues. His decision also raises the issue of whether or not a college education is appropriate or fair compensation for all NCAA revenue-producing athletes.

***Different academic standards and ethical conduct exist for revenue producing student-athletes.***

The central issue for black athletes (and white athletes as well) is dealing with an essentially corrupt and exploitive, "amateur" athletic system. Given the existing contradiction between the NCAA's mission of athletics as education versus the reality of revenue producing college athletics as big business, and the competitive marketplace for superior athletic talent, I believe it can be categorically said that every big-time athletic program violates NCAA rules or university policy. Simply put, different academic standards and ethical conduct exist for revenue producing student-athletes and their athletic departments versus regular students and their respective academic departments. By sustaining the fiction of the amateur athlete, a flourishing "black market" or underground economy exists for exceptional high school athletes involving school alumni, scouts, agents, runners, athletic shoe companies, high school coaches and high school administrators. Because many superior high school athletes are black and poor, and have attended academically deficient high schools, this means the interested university will need "help" in recruiting an athlete, admitting the athlete as a student to the university and keeping the athlete eligible for athletic participation and enrolled in school.

Perhaps the greatest irony of this morally bankrupt system for black athletes and their parents is how the work of largely poor black athletes, who dominate the top revenue producing football and basketball programs, finances the almost exclusively middle class white "minor" sports programs, million dollar plus coach's salaries, and extremely generous athletic department administration budgets.

**Radical Reform or Continued Corruption?**

By fostering the widening contradiction between the educational mission of the university and a for-profit sports entertainment enterprise on their college campuses, college officials have opened the door wide for the exploitation of revenue producing athletes. They have created a hypocritical system that allows corruption, dishonesty, and unfair dealing to be the rule. The cynical "bottom line" that justifies this state of affairs is that it is cheaper for the NCAA's member schools to maintain this dishonest and corrupt system rather than compete in the open market for athletic talent, much like professional sports teams do.

It is apparent that the present system of college revenue producing sport needs radical change. I would propose a college sports system that allows the top fifty or so schools to have legitimate professional football and basketball teams with a major caveat being the athlete having a range of choices as to how he or she will be paid, for their athletic labor. These choices would range from access to a guaranteed legitimate college education to cash payments or salaries. Athletes and their parents would select the various compensation plans and sign a binding contract with the school. Provisions could include modifying the compensation plan as the athlete career emerges. For example, an athlete could choose a guaranteed seven year scholarship as a high school senior but after his sophomore year, because he has a good chance at a professional career, could elect to take cash payments and focus on training for his sport, much like Olympic athletes do. In this scheme athletes could attend trade schools or enter apprentice programs, the cost of which would be part of their compensation package. Similarly athletes could elect non-academic courses of study at the university or other post-secondary schools.

The thrust of the above general scheme is to introduce a notion of honesty and fair dealing in revenue producing college sport. Given the relationship revenue producing college sports programs (football and basketball) have with the NFL and NBA, where the colleges are the developmental (minor) leagues for the pros, most high school athletes need to play college ball to sufficiently develop their athletic skills to play in the NFL and NBA. Professional football and basketball don't bear the cost of supporting minor leagues to develop talent and the colleges, under their present system, have access to a cost-free athletic labor pool. Those athletes who possess the athletic skill to play professionally should not be penalized or compromised by needing to go through the charade of being a student athlete. And they should not be forced to provide a college with three or four years of athletic labor before they have the opportunity to enter the pros.

In the present system, the vast majority of revenue producing athletes' athletic careers end in college; *less than one percent of Division IA athletes gain a professional team roster slot.* After four years of athletic labor, most walk away from their university without a college education or worthwhile degree, carrying only memories. Paraphrasing an old saying, "memories and a dollar bill will get you a cup of coffee."

Note: Subsequent to writing this article I read *Underpaid Professionals: Commercialism and Conflict in Big-Time College Sports* by Andrew Zimbalist, Princeton University Press, 1990. Zimbalist's and my analyses of revenue producing college sport coincide to a remarkable degree. He has produced an extremely thorough and detailed analysis of college revenue sport and an excellent book. I would recommend it highly to anyone interested in big-time college sport, the rampant contradictions inherent in it and the almost frightening patterns of racism, gender exploitation, cronyism, political boosterism, and exploitation of many of our finest athletes.

# Backlash against Title IX: An End Run around the Female Athletes[2]

BY ANDREW ZIMBALIST
*CHRONICLE OF HIGHER EDUCATION,* MARCH 3, 2000

After an initial burst of progress following its passage, in 1972, Title IX did little to promote gender equity in intercollegiate athletics during the 1980's. But the 1988 Civil Rights Restoration Act and subsequent court cases reinvigorated the progress of women in sports during the 1990's. The share of women among all intercollegiate athletes increased from 33.4 percent in 1990–91 to 39.9 percent in 1997–98.

Although such growth marks substantial improvement, women still have a long road to travel before they attain equity in college sports. During 1997–98 in Division I, women accounted for 41 percent of all athletics-scholarship money, 40 percent of all athletes, 33 percent of all sports' operating expenditures, 30 percent of recruitment spending, and 27 percent of base salaries for head coaches. Female athletes still play in inferior facilities, stay in lower-caliber hotels on the road, eat in cheaper restaurants, benefit from smaller promotional budgets, and have fewer assistant coaches.

Cedric W. Dempsey, the National Collegiate Athletic Association's president, assessed the status of gender equity in college sports last October: "Improvements are being made, but being made much too slowly . . . we must continue to add programs for women and dedicate more resources to women's programs on our campuses at a faster rate."

Yet some individuals and groups think that the progress toward gender equity is too rapid. The Center for Individual Rights, the Independent Women's Forum, and supporters of collegiate wrestling are pressing the presidential candidates, the courts, and other authorities to reinterpret Title IX or to change the law. They argue that it is wrong to cap the number of participants in some men's sports, or to eliminate some men's sports altogether, simply to meet quantitative standards dictated by Title IX.

---

2. Article by Andrew Zimbalist from *The Chronicle of Higher Education*. 

I sympathize with those who would prefer to see more opportunities for male athletes. But it is unrealistic to think that expanding women's sports alone—while leaving men's sports untouched—will be sufficient to achieve gender equity in the near or intermediate future. The problem, of course, is money.

In any given year, only about a dozen of the 973 colleges and universities in the N.C.A.A. have athletics programs that run a true surplus. The accounting practices of college sports are too tangled for me to elucidate that assertion in any detail here. Suffice it to note that the University of Michigan—which perennially ranks in the top 20 in football and men's basketball—has a football stadium with a capacity of 111,000 that has sold out every game since the mid-1980's, and earns more than $5 million annually in licensing revenues; yet the university ran a reported $2.5-million deficit in its athletics program last year.

Thus, unless higher-education institutions, state governments, and students are willing to further subsidize intercollegiate athletics programs at the expense of other educational activities, some redistribution of resources within athletics must occur. The critical question, and what everyone appears to be arguing about, is: Where should the money come from and where should it go?

The Title IX critics claim that men are being shafted. It's true that some men's teams have had their number of players capped, and a few men's sports at some institutions have been eliminated. But the larger picture does not show significant net losses for male athletes.

Hardest hit has been male wrestling. Even so, the number of colleges and universities sponsoring male wrestling teams fell only from 264 in 1993–94 to 246 in 1997–98, a modest decline of 6.8 percent. Some institutions have limited the number of "walk-ons," or nonscholarship players, in football and other men's sports, but the average Division I football team still has 103 players.

Over all, from 1978 to 1996 the total number of men's teams in all three N.C.A.A. divisions, in fact, increased by 74. After falling 12 percent from 1985 to 1996, the number of male athletes grew 6 percent in the last three years. In 1997–98, 203,686 male and 135,110 female athletes played college sports.

The Title IX detractors argue that it is both understandable and acceptable for male sports to receive greater resources because men's basketball and football produce the net revenues to finance the other sports. But that argument ignores several critical facts.

First, besides basketball and football, all men's sports—wrestling, squash, swimming, tennis, track and field, and the like—lose money, just like women's sports. If a market criterion were applied, any one of them could be subject to reduction or elimination.

Second, both Title IX and the courts' interpretation of it make clear that market forces should not be allowed to alter the goal of gender equity. Indeed, college sports programs happily enjoy numerous tax benefits, as well as the privilege of not paying salaries to their athletes, on the grounds that they are sponsoring amateur activities. It is duplicitous for colleges and universities to accept the fruits of amateurism for men's sports and then invoke business principles when it comes to financing women's sports. By the precepts of amateurism and the prevailing campus ethos, resources should be equally available to both men and women.

Third, although the absolute measures of women's participation and scholarship support are higher at Division I-A institutions, the relative measures—the share of resources going to women—are lower than they are at Division I-AAA (programs without football) and Division 11 institutions. Thus, the big-time college programs of Division I-A are no closer to meeting established gender-equity standards.

Most important, we have other, more attractive options for promoting gender equity—without diminishing or eliminating men's sports. Resources are available, if we are just willing to look for them.

For starters, men's basketball and football programs currently receive extravagant amounts of money. Although the base salaries for men's coaches—to which women's coaches' salaries are compared—are normally in the range of $125,000 to $200,000, total compensation packages for men's coaches on the leading teams routinely reach from $700,000 to $1.4 million.

Those salaries have no rhyme or reason, and soar well beyond what a competitive market would offer. What free market would pay strikingly similar total salaries to the coaches on the top three dozen football and men's basketball teams when the average revenue generated by a Division I-A football team is 2.7 times that of a Division I-A basketball team? And what market would pay a Division I-A football coach roughly the same total salary as a National Football League team coach, when an average N.F.L. team generates 10 times the revenue of an average Division I-A football team?

Such questions lead to another: Would it be too radical to require that a head coach's compensation package not exceed that of the university president? Such a reform would save dozens of institutions in the neighborhood of $1 million enough to finance two Division I swimming-and-diving teams, or one ice-hockey team.

**The 10 institutions where women receive the most aid, proportionally**

| | Female athletes | | Scholarships | | |
|---|---|---|---|---|---|
| Institution, NCAA division | Number | Proportion of total | Women's budget | Proportion of total | Difference |
| Drake U, 1-AA | 94 | 31.0% | $1,037,543 | 59.4% | + 28.3 |
| Morehead State U (KY), 1-AA | 105 | 29.4 | 351,681 | 52.0 | + 22.6 |
| Saint Peter's C, 1-AA | 102 | 31.8 | 1,200,337 | 53.6 | + 21.9 |
| Robert Morris C (PA), 1-AA | 104 | 33.8 | 572,407 | 54.3 | + 20.6 |
| U of Dayton, 1-AA | 124 | 37.9 | 871,467 | 58.1 | + 20.2 |
| Canisius C, 1-AA | 148 | 33.9 | 591,176 | 51.9 | + 18.1 |
| Saint John's U (NY), 1-AA | 142 | 34.6 | 1,754,827 | 52.5 | + 17.8 |
| U of San Diego, 1-AA | 143 | 36.7 | 1,118,510 | 53 | + 16.4 |
| U of Illinois, Chicago, 1-AAA | 95 | 41.9 | 794,650 | 58.0 | + 16.2 |
| Jacksonville U, 1-AA | 127 | 32.7 | 1,025,945 | 48.3 | + 15.5 |

Source: "Correction to athletics scholarships: Proportions for female athletes." *Chronicle of Higher Education*, April 21, 2000.

Another option? We could reduce the number of men's coaches in certain sports. The average Division I-A football team carries more than 10 assistant coaches. Cutting three of those coaches, each with an average salary of over $60,000 plus benefits and perquisites, would save enough to support a Division I-A college tennis team.

We should also ask: Why do Division I-A football teams need 85 scholarship players as, according to N.C.A.A. rules, they are allowed today? Only 11 players are on the field at a time. Even with three separate platoons—with different players for offense, defense, and special teams and a punter and place-kicker—a team needs only 35 players. N.F.L. teams have only 45 man rosters, with reserve squads of seven players.

| The 10 institutions where women receive the least aid, proportionally | | | | | |
|---|---|---|---|---|---|
| | Female athletes | | Scholarships | | |
| Institution, NCAA division | Number | Proportion of total | Women's budget | Proportion of total | Difference |
| Miami U (OH), 1-A | 264 | 43.9% | $990,228 | 30.7% | –13.2 |
| Murray State U, 1-AA | 144 | 41.5 | 398,676 | 29.2 | –12.3 |
| U of Oregon, 1-A | 254 | 48.8 | 1,389,812 | 36.8 | –11.9 |
| U of Kansas, 1-A | 375 | 51.2 | 1,432,745 | 40.8 | –10.4 |
| Weber State U, 1-AA | 161 | 44.1 | 409,501 | 34.2 | –9.9 |
| Alcom State U, 1-AA | 106 | 41.6 | 329,495 | 31.7 | –9.9 |
| Temple U, 1-A | 264 | 49.7 | 1,625,915 | 40.3 | –9.4 |
| Califonia State U, Fresno, 1-A | 273 | 50.4 | 894,522 | 41.1 | –9.3 |
| Villanova U, 1-AA | 269 | 49.2 | 1,824,663 | 40.6 | –8.6 |
| U of Colorado, Boulder, 1-AA | 139 | 41.7 | 1,350,830 | 33.1 | –8.6 |

Source: "Correction to athletics scholarships: Proportions for female athletes." *Chronicle of Higher Education*, April 21, 2000.

College coaches will maintain that they need more players than N.F.L. teams because of injuries, When an N.F.L. player is hurt, the team adds a player. College football does not have the same flexibility, the coaches say.

But most Division I-A teams carry 20 to 50 walk-ons, bringing their total rosters to well over 100. Why couldn't the number of scholarships be reduced to 60, saving each institution $350,000 or more-approximately the budget of a Division I wrestling team?

Finally, a long shot but one worth pursuing: Major League Baseball teams spend nearly $10-million each on their minor league and player-development systems. NFL and NBA teams don't have minor leagues; colleges do it for them. The N.C.A.A. also cooperates with the leagues in player-draft and eligibility regulations. Is there any reason why the NFL and NBA should not be contributing to the player-development programs at U. S. colleges?

I am heartened that Cedric Dempsey has issued public declarations that the progress of Title IX is too slow. When the N.C.A.A. strongly supports or objects to a proposal, it usually devotes resources to ensure its success or failure. From 1972 to 1974, for instance, it spent $300,000 lobbying against the full implementation of Title IX. In 1976, it invested additional funds into challenging Title IX in the courts. I hope that, this time around, the N.C.A.A. will convert its words into actions on behalf of Title IX.

Kimberly Schuld is the manager for special projects at the Independent Women's Forum. She asserts that implementation of Title IX has created a quota system and that colleges are starting "women's programs like bowling, squash, and tiddlywinks to say they have more women's programs and are in compliance."

Ms. Schuld's sarcasm to the contrary, women have shown that they are interested in participating in intercollegiate sports when the opportunities exist. At present, more than two million girls play interscholastic sports in high school—more than enough to supply enthusiastic players for larger numbers of women's teams in college. Attendance at women's sporting contests is growing every year, as are television ratings.

Until we support women's college sports at similar levels to those of the men—and for as long as a generation—we won't be able to assess their long-run potential. In the meantime, people who are concerned by the modest shrinking of men's sports should think less about taking resources away from female athletes and more about resources that are wasted at all levels of college athletics.

# College Athletes Deserve Some Equity[3]

BY CRAIG T. GREENLEE
*BLACK ISSUES IN HIGHER EDUCATION,* APRIL 27, 2000

In college sports, it seems that everybody gets paid except the athlete. That's a raw deal. The players provide the labor that produces winning teams, which in turn, generates heightened fan interest. As a result, football stadiums and basketball arenas are filled to capacity, translating into fatter operating budgets for the athletic powers.

The money trail doesn't end there. Here's a sampling:

- University of Florida football coach Steve Spurrier earns $2 million a year. Perks include performance bonuses (for his teams winning conference titles and going to bowl games), a clothing allowance, money for radio and television shows, a sportswear contract and two free cars—one for the coach, the other for Mrs. Spurrier.
- Tennessee women's basketball coach Pat Summitt doesn't fare badly either. Summitt's $500,000 a year income breaks down into a $175,000 base salary, $150,000 for radio and television shows, a $125,000 sports apparel contract, plus a $50,000 retention bonus.
- Tulsa basketball coach Bill Self got a sweet deal after his team fell one win short of advancing to this year's Final Four of the National Collegiate Atheletic Association tournament. He turned down an offer from the University of Nebraska that would have paid him anywhere from $800,000 to $1 million annually. Self, however, is being well compensated for staying put. He's now making $650,000—a whopping $300,000 raise—and for good measure, the school tossed in a $1 million annuity that kicks in if he stays with the program for five more years.
- Shoe contracts are becoming a regular source of income at most of the major colleges. Schools don't usually reveal how much they make from shoe contracts. But that's not the case at the University of North Carolina, Chapel Hill, which has a five-year, $7.1 million contract with Nike.

---

3. Article by Craig T. Greenlee from *Black Issues in Higher Education* April 27, 2000. 

Clearly, big-time college sports means big business. Last year, the payouts for football teams playing in bowl games ranged from $750,000 to $13 million.

Last fall, the NCAA cut a new deal with CBS for TV rights fees to air exclusive broadcasts all NCAA men's basketball tournament games. That contract is worth $6.2 billion and has been extended to the year 2013.

Hey, that's free enterprise, the stuff that made America what it is. But there's still a big problem with this scenario—the athletes are systematically barred from getting into the cash flow cycle.

The NCAA prohibits college athletes from earning money based on their status as amateurs. Coaches can do commercials and nobody questions their integrity or sense of fair play. For athletes, that's a no-no, one that could jeopardize their eligibility and ultimately cause them to be banned from further collegiate competition.

College athletes are at the mercy of ancient rules governing amateurism. Cases involving Chris Porter, Erick Barkley and Darnell Autry provide strong evidence of how college athletes are financially exploited by NCAA edicts:

- Porter, a senior and star basketball player at Auburn University, was ruled ineligible in late February after he admitted taking $2,500 from someone representing a sports agent. Porter used the money to keep his mother from being evicted from her home. He appealed, but the suspension held up, ending Porter's college career a week before the start of the NCAA tournament.
- Barkley, a highly regarded sophomore basketball player at St. John's University, was suspended twice by the NCAA this past season for receiving improper benefits.

  The first suspension resulted from him trading vehicles with a friend of the family. The second suspension came when it was discovered that an organization that Barkley played for paid his tuition while he attended prep school at Maine Central Institute. Barkley was reinstated, but the NCAA ruled he would have to pay back $3,500 of his $22,000 tuition which was paid for by Riverside Church of New York.

  Since the end of St. John's season, Barkley has decided to leave school and enter this year's National Basketball Association draft.
- In the summer of '96, Autry, a theater major who also played football for Northwestern University, was prohibited by NCAA rules from getting paid to appear in a movie to be shot in Italy.

  Autry challenged the ruling and the case went to court, but as things turned out, it was a split decision. The court ruled that

> Autry could work, but could not receive any pay because of his amateur status.
>
> For other college students who aren't on full athletic scholarships, that would never happen. They would be allowed to work and be paid whatever the going wage is.

Athletes having jobs has become a hot topic in college sports in recent years. And in '99, it seemed that the NCAA made a genuine attempt to provide some fiscal leeway, passing legislation allowing athletes to earn up to $2,000 during the school year working part-time jobs.

In principle, it's a step in the right direction, a move to be applauded. In reality, it's a cruel joke.

Given the demands of being a college athlete, putting in 20 hours a week at a part-time job is not very practical. The hours athletes would spend working at a job are already spoken for.

Typically, they already spend that much time every week in team meetings, practices and traveling to out-of-town games. And depending on the sport, the time demands during the offseason aren't that much different from the actual season.

***College athletes should be paid some kind of reasonable stipend, . . . which should be made part of the awarded scholarship.***

That's why college athletes should be paid some kind of reasonable stipend, perhaps $200 a month, which should be made part of the awarded scholarship. Since they don't have the time to work, it's the only way they can receive money without breaking any NCAA rules. With a stipend in place, coaches and athletic administrators wouldn't be burdened with monitoring for potential abuses by school alumni and/or booster club members.

It's the fair thing to do, especially for those athletes who come from low-income families.

True, athletes who are on a "full ride" have all the basics covered for school: tuition, books and room and board. Even so, the scholarship does not include a spending money allowance to help cover incidental expenses such as laundry and bath items or being able to go to the movies or buy a hamburger and french fries.

The NCAA uses the term "student-athletes" in referring to the folks who play collegiate sports. They're supposed to be just like the rest of the student body, the only difference is that they play competitive sports.

It's clear, however, that student-athletes aren't treated the same as their non-jock counterparts. A chemistry student going to school on an academic scholarship would not be prevented from working part-time to help pay for incidentals. The same is true for all other majors who do not play sports for the school. Why is it that athletes can't get the same deal?

Sheer greed.

College sports officials need to end their shameful hypocrisy and start giving back to those who help make the institutions NCAA powerhouses. The athletes deserve some financial consideration in helping to build a multi-billion dollar industry.

It's the right thing to do.

# Inside the NBA: Springing a League[4]

BY JACKIE MACMULLAN AND DAVID SABINO
*SPORTS ILLUSTRATED*, APRIL 10, 2000

NBA execs say they plan a minor league for 2001, but they're suspiciously vague about it.

From the beginning the details have been hazy. The NBA, which doesn't undertake any venture halfheartedly, began discussing in February its intention to start a developmental league in 2001. NBA officials said there would be eight teams, maybe 10. Last Friday deputy commissioner Russ Granik, who usually speaks with crystal clarity on the league's plans, was vague when pressed for particulars. What cities will be getting franchises? "Well, we're not completely sure," Granik said. "We wouldn't go into a market like San Diego or Cincinnati or Pittsburgh. We'd be looking at smaller cities, with a few hundred thousand people."

How much will the players be paid? Unclear. How will they be assigned to teams? Unclear. "You have to remember," Granik said, "we're in very preliminary stages."

When commissioner David Stern decides to pursue a deal, he knows only one speed: breakneck. When he determined that money could be made on the women's game, he rammed the WNBA down the throats of the NBA's sponsors and fans and drove the ABL out of business. When Stern decided that his league needed to do more with the Internet, he threw his energy into *NBA.com*, spending most of All-Star weekend hyping his sport's on-line potential while virtually ignoring the coming-out party of his new superstar, Vince Carter.

So if Stern is hell-bent on having a minor league up and running next year, why are so many issues unresolved? Could it be that the NBA's latest project is merely a ploy to squeeze a better deal out of CBA owner Isiah Thomas, as a number of NBA sources suggested last week?

When Thomas approached Stern last year with his plan to buy the CBA, spruce up its image and develop a formal association with the NBA, Stern said thanks but no thanks. Thomas, who sparred with Stern as president of the players' union from 1988 to '94, decided to buy the CBA anyway. He figured that sooner or later the CBA

4. Reprinted courtesy of *Sports Illustrated*: "Inside the NBA: Springing a League" by Jackie MacMullan and David Sabino, *Sports Illustrated*, April 10, 2000. 

would formalize its role as the NBA's minor league. "I don't want to fight with the NBA," Thomas says. "I believe there's an opportunity here for the CBA to service the NBA as well as the NCAA. If we all put our heads together, we can work it out."

Granik insists the NBA isn't out to bury Thomas. "I continue to have conversations with Isiah," Granik says. "I'm hoping we'll reach an agreement." But asked if a deal with the CBA would eliminate the need for a developmental league, Granik says, "Not necessarily. I envision blending the two."

The proposed developmental league was a hot topic at the McDonald's All-American Game on March 29 at Boston's FleetCenter, where five players who are considering the jump from high school to the pros were on display: forwards Darius Miles of East St. Louis, Ill., Darius Rice of Jackson, Miss., and Gerald Wallace of Childersburg, Ala.; and guards Jerome Harper of Columbia, S.C., and DeShawn Stevenson of Fresno.

Miles, a wiry 6'8" small forward with exceptional open-floor skills who is projected as a Top 5 pick if he comes out, considers "the junior varsity," as he calls the projected league, a great idea. "I wouldn't need something like that, but it would help guys like Korleone Young, who went out too soon, got messed up and had no options," Miles says. (Young, a high school player who was picked in the second round by the Pistons in 1998, was released after one season and is now in the IBL.)

"No high school kid is ready to go to the pros, but that doesn't mean I won't do it," Miles continues. "I think I can hit a nice 10 to 15 points a night (in the NBA) right now, with a couple of blocks and some steals. I don't think I'm ready yet to be Vince or Kobe and knock down 30 or 40. But I figure I've got time for that."

Both Granik and Thomas insist they don't want the developmental league to be a haven for high school kids who come out early but fail to make an NBA roster. "As an Afro-American I feel I have an obligation to show some responsibility," Thomas says. "I could never say to these kids, 'C'mon, play basketball. Forget about being educated.'"

But could Granik ban high school kids from the new league? To be determined. Would someone like Pacers forward Jonathan Bender, who has potential but can't crack Indiana's lineup, be welcome in the league, Russ? Don't know. And one more thing: If this is all happening next year, why haven't Stern & Co. discussed it with the players' union, which has no interest in allowing its members to be farmed out at the whim of management?

"Sooner or later they'd have to come to us, because we'd have to sign off on it," says union executive director Billy Hunter. "But we're not buying into anything right now. Our position is clear: If young players don't have the talent to be (in the NBA), then don't draft them."

# Base Hits: There Are Major-League Benefits in the Minors[5]

BY MATTHEW J. BERNTHAL AND PETER J. GRAHAM
*MARKETING NEWS*, OCTOBER 25, 1999

You go to a minor-league baseball game and your home team plays horribly, losing to their cross-state rivals. Topping it all off, the restrooms and stadium weren't particularly clean. However, you leave the game feeling satisfied with the experience. How can this be?

If a physical product performed as miserably as your team did on this outing, there is no doubt you would be dissatisfied. Further, the relationship between product performance and satisfaction is not unique to physical, tangible goods. Indeed, if some service goods—for example, a symphony orchestra—performed as poorly as your team, you would be dissatisfied. So why is minor-league baseball different? How can a team perform poorly yet still satisfy customers? The answer can be found by examining the value and service quality literature and applying it to the unique experience that is minor-league baseball.

It is generally accepted that satisfaction is positively related to perceived value. To determine what constitutes value in minor-league baseball, we collected data at four minor-league games. Difficulties arose, however, as a surprising 96% of spectators at the four games judged the games a "good value." Value was considered high even by those judging attributes such as employee friendliness and stadium and restroom cleanliness as relatively poor, and yes, value was considered high even when the home team lost. Quite simply, we didn't find enough spectators dissatisfied with the experience's value.

Several factors contribute to minor-league baseball's leaving a satisfaction record most marketers only dream of. First, value can be conceptualized as the consumer's overall assessment of a product's utility based on perceptions of what is gained and what is given. Minor-league baseball's utility is uniformly high: For meager ticket prices—usually in the $5-to-$8 range—those seeking to entertain family, friends or simply themselves gain a great deal. Spectators are treated to several hours of relaxed entertainment which

5. Reprinted with permission from *Marketing News*, published by the American Marketing Association, by Matthew J. Brenthal and Peter J. Graham, October 25, 1999, vol. 33, page 39.

includes, but is not limited to, the game itself. For example, between-innings entertainment, such as a race around the bases between a mascot and a child from the stands, provides spectators with added value. Entertaining sound effects like breaking glass on a foul ball keep spectators chuckling during the game, while post-game entertainment may include fireworks or a music concert. Add those factors up, and it becomes easy to see why the vast majority of minor-league baseball consumers consider it a good value; in other words, the total entertainment package the consumers receive vastly overshadows the low ticket price.

A second aspect is that consumers tend to judge a product's value against substitutable goods. Minor-league baseball hits a home run here as well. As a member of the broad "family-friendly entertainment" category for example, a minor-league ticket can be purchased for less than the cost of a movie, and the consumer is entertained for a significantly greater length of time. A couple or group can go to a minor-league game, be entertained for several hours, have the opportunity for conversation and eat for less than the cost of dining out in a restaurant. Further, the minor leagues beat the major leagues as well in terms of value. Many fans perceive the minors as a purer form of baseball than the majors, with the game seemingly less "corrupted" by money and greed and the players more grateful for the opportunity to simply play baseball. In addition, many of the minor-league entertainment benefits described earlier are nonexistent at major league events. Minor leagues sell entertainment, while the majors sell baseball and the uncertainty of game outcome. These facts, combined with escalating major-league ticket prices, declare the minors the clear winner in terms of value.

***Many fans perceive the minors as a purer form of baseball than the majors.***

A third reason for the exceedingly high levels of satisfaction revolves around disconfirming expectations. The vast majority of spectators at minor-league games clearly experience positive disconfirmation. Low cost, especially compared to substitutable entertainment and realizing that they are watching minor-league players both function to keep fan expectations in check. When players perform at less-than-admirable levels and the facilities are less-than-impressive, fans take comfort in the "total entertainment" package they are receiving for their money, and the actual perceived experience exceeds expectations despite these shortcomings. Major-league baseball, on the other hand, doesn't enjoy the same luxury; major-league prices have brought about major-league expectations that are becoming increasingly difficult to meet. New stadiums, with their ever-expanding luxury suites and club seats, rising player salaries and the like, have led to ticket prices which have driven many spectators—especially families—out of the market. These prices have led those who do attend major-league games to do so with expectations far exceeding those found in minor-league ballparks. Most major-league spectators expect their entertainment dollar to be rewarded by good play, clean, impressive facilities and the like.

Higher expectations, however, lead to more opportunity for dissatisfaction, and major-league baseball needs to take note of this. Could it be that the minor-leagues actually have something to teach the majors? Major-league players might cringe at the thought of being sent down to the minors, but major league fans might find the minors to be the true home of "big-league" entertainment.

# IV. The Good, the Great, and the Ugly

*Michael Jordan of the Chicago Bulls during the first round of the playoffs against the Miami Heat, April 24, 1992.*

# *Editor's Introduction*

Since the earliest days of the 20th century, when tobacco companies were enclosing baseball cards in their packages and Jim Thorpe was winning gold medals at the 1912 Olympic Games, athletes have been role models and heroes for countless Americans. That distinction is often deserved, as in the case of individuals like Joe Louis, Jackie Robinson, Michael Jordan, and Joe Montana, who have displayed exceptional skill and fortitude in their stellar careers. Too often, however, the behavior of professional athletes and officials prompts more headshaking than applause, as millionaire ball players turn criminal or those running a sport are suspected of corruption. Section IV considers some of these individuals, in all of their glory and shame.

The articles that open the section explore the goodness or greatness of several athletes from two different perspectives. In "The Greatest Show on Earth" *Sports Illustrated* columnist Rick Reilly looks at Tiger Woods, who had arguably the best year of any golfer in the history of the PGA tour in 2000. By reflecting on the manner in which Woods dominated his opponents and comparing him to other sports legends, Reilly urges readers to savor his achievements, the likes of which they may not see again in their lifetimes. The next article, David Scott's "Touched by Greatness," considers the charity work done by Jordan, Wayne Gretzky, and John Elway, which the writer portrays as another manifestation of the heroism they displayed during their hall-of-fame careers. They and athletes like them continue to impress their fans, even after retirement, by donating their time and money to the communities that have supported them over the years. In "God bless Lance Armstrong," Heather Lende contemplates the joys and struggles of cycling while drawing inspiration from Armstrong's first Tour De France victory after his bout with cancer.

While the players above have made headlines for outstanding performance and/or generosity, others have become notorious for far more dubious achievements. In "A Season of Shame," Mark Starr and Allison Samuels review the cases of numerous athletes, such as Ray Lewis and Rae Caruth, who have been suspected of or jailed for serious crimes during the past couple of years. The writers examine the culture that nurtures and produces these individuals, both on and off the field, and examine how professional leagues like the NFL are dealing with this situation. Sometimes, however, a sport's problems are more systemic, as Jack Newfield and Wallace Mathews assert in "Boxing Reformers Should Go for KO." According to the writers, it is the boxing officials in such organizations as the IBF and World Boxing Council, rather than the fighters themselves, who are corrupt; allegedly, they sell rankings to determine matchups, and appoint dishonest judges and referees to officiate fights. Newfield and Matthews suggest that authority should rest instead in the hands of the state boxing commissions and a pool of sports writers, who could better ensure the integrity of the sport and the quality of the matches.

# The Greatest Show on Earth[1]

BY RICK REILLY
*SPORTS ILLUSTRATED*, AUGUST 28, 2000

It's a strange job, traipsing about, typing sports. You forget how to tingle. Your Amaze-o-Meter gets stuck on empty. A comeback to win the Super Bowl? *Yawn, scribble.* A 9.9 to win the gold? *Scribble, yawn.* Almost 220 mph on that last lap? *Yawn, yawn.*

Then along comes Tiger Woods, and a job becomes a privilege. I would pogo from Bangor to Birmingham to see Woods play. I would wear spike heels, a see-through muumuu and RuPaul's curlers if it were the only way through the gate. I ought to buy my dad a box of cigars for having me the year that he did.

We're lucky. All of us. We're alive when the single most dominating athlete in 70 years is at his jaw-dropping best. Bathe in it. Wallow in it. Savor it. Take notes. Get video. Save newspapers. Your grandkids will want details.

Michael Jordan? This guy is better. Jordan had teammates. Woods is out there by himself. Jordan beat guys one-on-one, one-on-two. Woods won last week's unforgettable PGA Championship at Valhalla one-on-149. What's more, Woods never got cheap calls from refs.

Woods is pureeing everybody, everywhere, every way—from miles ahead and from two behind, as he was on Sunday with 12 holes to play. How many guys are good enough to win a major playing off cart paths on the last two holes? He thumps great players, and he survives the guy pulling gold monkeys out of his ear. Staring into the biggest upset since Colts-Jets, he snuffed out a toy pit bull named Bob May with a mile of must-make putts. All he did was birdie eight of 13 holes, including the first playoff hole. You can't Buster Douglas Tiger Woods. He stuffs every Cinderella back into the pumpkin.

Woods is the most amazing performer I've ever seen, and I've seen Ali, Gretzky, Jordan, Montana and Nicklaus. What Woods is doing is so hard it's like climbing Everest in flip-flops. Performing heart transplants in oven mitts. The four major championships have been played 344 times, and Woods now holds or shares the scoring record in all four of them? That's *sick.*

---

1. Reprinted courtesy of *Sports Illustrated* "The Greatest Show on Earth" by Rick Reilly, August 28, 2000. 

Woods's adjusted scoring average this year is 67.86, which would be a record by about a mile if it holds up for the rest of the season. Before Woods put up his 68.43 last year, only Greg Norman (68.81) in 1994 and Nick Price (68.98) in '97 had broken 69. Since the PGA Tour came up with the adjusted scoring average in 1988, the largest margin of victory—other than Woods's .74 last year—was Norman's .58 of a stroke. This year Woods figures to lead by 1.53 strokes. That's, what, 163% better than the Shark's margin?

You're sick of hearing about Tiger Woods. You're going to hear more. He has more than twice as much jing as the next guy on the PGA Tour money list. He has more than triple the points of the next guy on the U.S. Ryder Cup list. He has more than twice as many points as the next guy in the World Golf Ranking. Muhammad Ali was great, but was he twice as great as Joe Frazier?

The grumps in the press tent keep trying to find a buzzkill in all this. *Hey, Nicklaus had to beat Gary Player and Tom Watson.* Hey, if Woods didn't exist, wouldn't Ernie Els be Player by now? Might not David Duval have a chance to be Watson? Brilliant careers are going around stuck on Woods's golf spikes.

*What do you have to shoot to win here?* Stuart Appleby was asked last Thursday.

"Tiger Woods," he said.

Go see this kid while you're breathing. Three straight majors? Not done in 47 years. Four of the last five majors? Not done, ever. Now he's leaning on the doorbell of something nobody thought would ever be done: the Grand Slam. Oh, yes, it is. If Woods wins the Masters next April, that *is* the Grand Slam. It's not the *continuous* Slam or the *asterisk* Slam, just the Grand Slam. He says so. I say so. Hell, sportswriters invented it; sportswriters make the rules. And don't give me Bobby Jones. Beating three guys named Nigel and two sheep at the British Amateur doesn't even compute.

Last Thursday at Valhalla, Woods and Jack Nicklaus were walking down the first fairway, their ears ringing from the roars. "Man, it's loud," Nicklaus said to Woods. "Thank God, I'm done playing. Now you get to deal with this the rest of your career."

As well he should.

# Touched by Greatness[2]

BY DAVID SCOTT
*SPORT,* NOVEMBER 1999

We were spoiled, you know. Spoiled rotten. Oh, sure, we tried to fully appreciate it all, but how could we, really? After all, isn't the best part of sports the memories? The moments frozen in time by the VCR, the Nikon or better yet, the mind. The ones that become more and more dramatic with each peek back. Endless, they seem. The Drive. The Shot. The Goal. Something out of nothing. Wins out of losses.

Suddenly, though, the music stopped. All at once, it seemed. First, Michael Jordan, then Wayne Gretzky and lastly John Elway. Can it be? Shouldn't they have consulted with each other? Couldn't they have staggered the announcements into neat, yearly segments? Gretzky could have gone first, no final title in sight, nothing left to prove. Then Elway, after he tried for three in a row. And lastly, Michael, because he still had the most left to give us.

We could have appreciated each one, praised each one, one at a time, in full, until the next announcement. But no. Boom. Boom. Boom. One calendar year, one five-month period. One-hundred and nine days and POOF! Goodbye, Michael. So long, Wayne. Later, John.

"It is unfortunate that we all retired at pretty much the same time," Jordan says. "But life and other things have to continue." And that's actually the one sweetener, the sorbet to the feast of moments they've given us, that we can take from being dumped three times in five months. These legends have been stars off the court as well. Each has used his fame, his name, to spread the wealth to those less blessed. What could be worth celebrating more than the acts of charity Jordan, Gretzky and Elway can continue to share? No more highlight reels? No problem.

"It gives you chills to see the kids' faces and their expressions and to see them enjoy a moment during a trying situation," says Jordan of his visits to The Ronald McDonald Houses in North Carolina. "I've been very fortunate to bring that kind of smile to someone who needs it."

---

2. Article by David Scott from *Sport* November 1999. 

Remember one thing: These are three of the greatest competitors in the history of sports. Competition doesn't leave your body like a cold. It remains, and some would say, intensifies. So they have to adjust. Find "new challenges." Set "new goals." Each conquered his domain. Who could be surprised that they have already prepared themselves for their second acts?

"That's my goal: to be better at my second career than I was at my first," says Elway. "First of all, you want to set the charitable foundation going in, you want to get it going while you're still playing because that's when you've got the platform to really do something and raise a lot of money. And then once you're done playing and you've got a little more time, that's when you can spend more time

***The sports career is incumbent mainly on what sports fans see and understand. The post-sports career relies mostly on what society sees and understands.***

focusing on it. I think it makes you feel good about what you're doing because it makes you feel good about yourself. You know you can help other people in situations because you have the platform."

What a powerful platform it can be. The sports career is incumbent mainly on what sports fans see and understand. The post-sports career relies mostly on what society sees and understands. A subtle difference, perhaps, but a difference nonetheless. "I'm not sure what society gains," Elway says. "I just know, looking at Wayne and Michael and what they did for their respective sports—not only were they great players, but they were great people too. The world of sports loses two great icons, but as far as society goes and what they can do, I think you'll be hearing about them for a long time. Michael Jordan and Wayne Gretzky will always be role models because they're good people."

Too humble to include himself, Elway fits right in with his own words. All three had the special ability to transcend any singular categorical grouping. They crossed racial and social lines and united many in something so simple: the act of playing.

For his part, Gretzky not only actively participates in charity events, he has first-hand experience in organizing one. As an enterprising 18-year old, Gretzky and a buddy organized a tennis tournament in his hometown of Brantford to raise funds for the nearby Canadian National Institute for the Blind. "It was a lot of fun, but at the end of the day we were $2,000 in the hole. My dad wrote a check for $3,000 so the charity would be up $1,000. My dad's still a big spokesman for CNIB today."

Gretzky also knows first-hand the emotional strain of dealing with a physical or mental disability. His aunt Ellen has Down's syndrome and was home-schooled. Today, Gretzky is involved with a revolutionary computer/video-conferencing apparatus called P.E.B.B.L.E.S (Providing Education By Bringing Learning Environment to Students). A communications device, it allows hospitalized children to take part in school, providing a link from the hospital to the classroom.

"I once had a classmate who had tuberculosis, and he had to miss an entire year of school," says Gretzky. "By doing this, the kids are

***"Sometimes athletes forget what you can do and how much your name associated with causes can be of benefit."*—Wayne Gretzky.**

able to stay in school and on top of their homework." Aside from lending his name to the project, Gretzky donates $1 for every item of his clothing line sold at The Bay stores across Canada. To date, his line has raised more than $130,000.

"Sometimes athletes forget what you can do and how much your name associated with causes can be of benefit," Gretzky says. "I think you first realize it once you have your own kids. I know my kids look up to people like John Elway and Michael Jordan, and until you see your kids actually idolizing other people, sometimes you kind of forget that there are a lot of kids out there who idolize you."

You just know Jordan doesn't pass a McDonald's without thinking of the children he has touched through his work with the Ronald McDonald House. There was the small boy named Carlton, who sat with Jordan during his auction and golf tournament. Jordan instructed the young boy to bid on a set of golf clubs on Jordan's behalf. "Ten-thousand," "11,000," came the bids, and finally the clubs were Jordan's for $12,000. Just imagine the look and the tears that came streaming down the boy's face when the clubs he thought were to be Jordan's were instead delivered to him. Jordan touched and was touched.

What of Elway's involvement with the Kempe Children's Foundation for abused children? One-million times more baffling than the zone blitz to Elway is the idea of beating a child. "It boggled my mind to see the way children were abused by their parents, especially thinking back to the relationship I had with my parents and the love and relationship I have with my kids," Elway says. "I don't understand why someone would abuse a child. But I think we've learned that it goes on, and we've raised the awareness that it occurs and hopefully we've prevented as many cases as we could. It's the kids and the relationship I have with the kids, even though I've never met most of them, to see their letters come in. It makes me feel pretty good." Elway touched and was touched.

Now they will continue with these and other charities. They will have business endeavors and family time. There will be television appearances and books. Help for those who ask and some who don't. They will continue to affect us in ways we never envisioned. Maybe better ways.

Retired? In a sense. But just beginning, in essence.

Spoiled, we are. Gloriously, lavishly and incomparably spoiled.

## Money for Something

BY ADAM HIRSHFIELD
*SPORT*, NOVEMBER 1999

It's not just about the money but also the unique ways in which athletes give back. Here's a list of interesting donations tied to on-field performance that will give anyone scoring at home an added incentive to pay attention:

| Athlete | $ per statistic | Charity |
|---|---|---|
| Andy Ashby, MLB | $100/strikeout | American Cancer Society |
| Peter Bondra, NHL | $100/standings point | Children's Inn at National Institute of Health |
| Shawn Bradley, NBA | $50/blocked shot | Bryan's House (kids with HIV and AIDS) |
| Doug Brien, NFL | $100/field goal | Big Brothers/Big Sisters of Southeast Louisiana |
| Rico Brogna, MLB | $100/RBI | Spondylitis Association of America |
| Kevin Brown, MLB | $1,000/win | Covenant House; Make-A-Wish Foundation; Jenesse Center (each) |
| Robert Burnett, NFL | $500/team sack | St. Vincent Hospital/Courage House |
| Tony Clark, MLB | $300/HR; $100/RBI ($20,000 minimum) | Detroit public schools |
| Ron Coomer, MLB | $125/extra-base hit | Children's Miracle Network |
| Sean Dawkins, NFL | $100/touchdown | Cancer Center of Children's Hospital |
| Brett Farvre, NFL | $150/rushing or passing TD | Boys and Girls Club of Green Bay |
| Sergei Fedorov, NHL | $91/Red Wings goal | Local charities |
| Mark Fields, NFL | $20/tackle and sack | A Child's Wish of Greater New Orleans |
| Cliff Floyd, MLB | $250/HR and stolen base | Reviving Baseball in Inner-cities (RBI) |
| Grant Fuhr, NHL | $500/win | ER at Cardinal Glennon Children's Hospital |
| Juan Gonzalez, MLB | $100/RBI | Reading, Writing, and RBIs |
| Kent Graham, NFL | $200/TD | Athletes in Action |
| Elvis Grbac, NFL | $2,000/team TD pass | Children's Mercy Hospital (Spina Bifida) |
| Trent Green, NFL | $200/team passing TD | Trent Green Family Foundation |
| Andre Hastings, NFL | $100/TD | Children's Hospital Cancer Center |

MLB = Major League Baseball; NBA = National Basketball Association; NFL = National Football League; NHL = National Hockey League

| Money for Something (cont.) | | |
|---|---|---|
| **Athlete** | **$ per statistic** | **Charity** |
| Bobby Higginson, MLB | $500/HR; $250/RBI | Disadvantaged children's charities |
| Sterling Hitchcock, MLB | $100/strikeout | The Good News Club |
| Trevor Hoffman, MLB | $200/save | National Kidney Foundation of Southern California |
| Dale Jarrett, NASCAR (Ford Credit) | $10,000/win; $7,500/ 2nd place; $500/3rd; $5,000/pole | Susan G. Komen Breast Cancer Foundation |
| Jeff Kent, MLB | $500/RBI | Women Driven; program benefitting female walk-on athletes at Cal-Berkeley |
| Mark Martin, NASCAR (Valvoline) | $5,000/win; $2,500/ pole; $20/lap lead | Big Brothers/Big Sisters of America |
| Keenan McCardell, NFL | $100/catch; $500/TD | Baptist Regional Cancer Institute for breast cancer initiatives |
| Jim McIlvaine, NBA | $25/blocked shot | Fred Hutchinson Cancer Research Center fund |
| Brian Moehler, MLB | $50/strikeout | American Heart Association |
| Alex Molden, NFL | $500/interception | Boys and Girls Club of New Orleans |
| Keith Poole, NFL | $100/TD | Cancer Center of Children's Hospital |
| Pete Sampras, ATP Tour | $100 or more/ace | Aces for Charity |
| Curt Schilling, MLB | $1,000/win; $100/ strikeout | Curt's Pitch for ALS (Lou Gehrig's Disease) |
| Kurt Schultz, NFL | $200/team interception | Meals on Wheels |
| Seattle Seahawks offensive line, NFL | $50/first down; $250/ offensive TD; $200/200-yard rushing game; $300/300-yard passing game; $3,000/300 yards total offense | Boyer Children's Clinic |
| Jimmy Smith, NFL | $100/catch; $500/TD | Wolfson Children's Hospital |
| Bernie Williams, MLB | $200/HR | Children's Health Fund |
| Dan Wilson, MLB | $250/caught base-stealer | First Place School |

ATP = Association of Tennis Professionals; MLB = Major League Baseball; NASCAR = National Association of Stock Car Racing; NBA = National Basketball Association; NFL = National Football League; NHL = National Hockey League

# God Bless Lance Armstrong[3]

BY HEATHER LENDE
*CHRISTIAN SCIENCE MONITOR,* JULY 24, 2000

The alarm goes off at five in the morning. My husband and I are cyclists, and just about every day until it snows we ride with our neighbor, Steve.

Before we head out, we drink sweet creamy coffee and talk about Lance Armstrong and the Tour De France. We talk about the hill climb where he encouraged his Italian rival to join him crossing the finish line. Though we've never met him, never even been in the same state, we are as proud of Lance as if he were one of us. We think he's great. He rode 125 miles that day. We're just going thirty this morning. "Piece of cake," my husband says.

Inspired, we head out the door, our cycling-shod toes up as we hobble over the gravel drive. I can hear Steve clipping into the pedals. We join him, warming up, until we reach Cemetery Hill, about a half mile at a 9% grade. Lance rode up 6000 feet in seven miles. He probably wouldn't even call this a hill. But it nearly finishes me every day. There's not a soul on the road, so we power up the middle. The men pull away, I stand up on the pedals, counting "one and two and one and two and . . ." to keep my pace steady. My heart is banging against my ribs and I'm gasping for air. I sit again reminding myself to pull, not push.

At the top I spin hard over the crest and head down, catching the men again. We coast to the highway and then begin our ride out along the river, through the Chilkat Valley. There are markers every mile indicating the mileage, but we know the way by heart: the clumps of trees, the rises and dips, the places where there's no shoulder and the ones with smooth new pavement. We even know everyone in the handful of pick-ups that pass us on their way out to work on a road construction job farther down the road.

We pull hard, taking short, strong strokes, smoothly transferring the lead from one to the next every thirty seconds or so. We are riding about 25 miles per hour. We'll hit thirty at a bend in the river where the wind picks up, but mostly we stay in the low twenties. And it's not easy.

---

3. This article first appeared in the electronic edition of *The Christian Science Monitor* on March 6, 1998, and is reproduced with permission. 

Steve says "they ride at 28 miles an hour when they're coasting." We know he's talking about Lance and his U.S. Postal Service teammates.

We pedal on, legs hurting, lungs bursting, holding ourselves still and smooth, keeping the cadence high and our upper bodies motionless. We are riding as hard and well as we can.

I know it sounds silly for three forty-something adults about as far from France and the cycling world as you can get, to ride like we do, for nothing really. Oh, we do have little races—four of five of us get together some Saturday or Sunday and race each other. There are no ribbons at the end and no crowds lining the route.

But there are moments. After a hard pull into the wind, when I tuck in behind the leaders, the draft from their bikes creates a lull; my legs no longer hurt and I'm suddenly flying along with no effort. It's quiet, and I have a second to look up, just as the sun hits the snow on the Cathedral Peaks—and I know that this is the peace that passes all understanding, and for just a moment (it'll be my turn to pull again too soon) I feel like I have touched the hem of God's robe.

The media makes a big deal out of Lance Armstrong's comeback. They speculate that he wanted to prove to himself and the world he could beat it.

I know it's a stretch to compare my little riding group with Tour De France champions, but I have cycled enough to know that Lance's comeback may have more to do with wanting to find that peace again, than winning.

So here's to you Lance—in the words of the old Irish blessing, which must have been conceived on a bicycle, "May the road rise up to meet you and the wind be always at your back."

# A Season of Shame[4]

BY MARK STARR AND ALLISON SAMUELS
*NEWSWEEK*, MAY 29, 2000

As he turned 25 years old last week in an Atlanta courtroom at his own murder trial, football star Ray Lewis wasn't looking much like a hero. Wearing a sober suit, he scribbled notes on a yellow legal pad and talked to his defense team, barely glancing at his two codefendants just 10 feet away. It was a humbling posture for Lewis, who last season had another great year for the Baltimore Ravens, leading the league in tackles, making the All-Pro team, enjoying a new $26 million contract. He'd been swaggering then, hitting the clubs in a full-length mink coat and a much longer limo, surrounded by worshipful friends. But the night of the Super Bowl last January, outside a club called the Cobalt Lounge, there was a confrontation and two men died. Lewis has pleaded not guilty. A defense attorney asked one prospective juror what his initial reaction was when he saw the news reports. "I said to myself, 'Oh, no—not another sports figure.' It was just something I was tired of."

So is everybody else: tired, alarmed, angry. We revere our sports heroes, pay them millions, build a good part of our culture around their exploits. Our children want to emulate them. We expect the world of them. Are these expectations unfair? Maybe. But one thing is sure: now more than ever, these athletes are crashing and burning in front of our eyes. The sports pages are full of crime, drug incidents and assaults on women. Lewis wasn't even the only Pro Bowler in court last week. Green Bay Packer star Mark Chmura was charged with sexually assaulting a drunken 17-year-old, a regular babysitter for his children, at a post-prom party. His attorney has filed a motion seeking to dismiss the charges. And former Carolina Panther receiver Rae Carruth was awaiting trial for allegedly arranging a fatal "hit" on his pregnant girlfriend. He has pleaded not guilty. In just the past year, some three dozen NFL athletes have been arrested, while a host of other sports figures have found trouble. Just last week skater Tonya Harding was sentenced to jail for assaulting her boyfriend with a hubcap; coach Bobby Knight almost lost his job for harassing his players and anyone else who annoyed him. When NFL owners sit down at their

4. Article by Mark Starr and Allison Samuels from *Newsweek* May 29, 2000. 

annual spring meeting this week, the issue of athletes' off-field travails will top the agenda. Says Tampa Bay Bucs coach Tony Dungy: "We're in a danger zone."

The recipe for trouble has always existed in professional sports: ill-prepared young kids ushered too quickly into the spotlight, bathed in adoration, showered with riches, surrounded by hangers-on. But the money and media attention has intensified the pace of it all. New York Knicks star Latrell Sprewell, once reviled for choking his coach, understands it well: "Things come at you so fast sometimes you don't know what to do. We're only human."

Much has been said, too, about an ever-growing sense of entitlement, fed by our sports-crazed culture. "We put these people on a pedestal and give them more than what is their due," says Lew Lyon, a Baltimore psychologist who works with pro athletes. "Everyone tells them how good they are, and they believe it. There's this sense that they're above it all." Among that chorus: the proverbial entourage, the moochers, sycophants and predators who bird-dog sports starts. Calvin Hill, the former Cowboys running back and father of the NBA superstar Grant, says athletes are especially vulnerable. "They don't have the intuition or the skepticism."

But while many players say their friends are an invaluable support system, for others the presence of a "posse" can bring the violence of the streets back into their lives. Sports has always had its share of athletes with humble backgrounds. But as the industry becomes ever more efficient in discovering and grooming talent, more and more kids are being plucked out of the projects and other rough neighborhoods. Leo Armbrust, a Roman Catholic priest and team chaplain screens college players for the Miami Dolphins. Of the 76 he interviewed this year, Father Armbrust says 27 had no connection to their biological fathers, seven had a member of their immediate family who had been shot and three had dads in prison—and that's just what was volunteered. "These young men are not from another planet," he says. "These are the times we

## Say It Ain't So, Guys

From the months leading up to training camp, on through the Super Bowl and up until last week, the 1999–2000 NFL season sometimes seemed more like a rerun of *Law & Order*. Some lowlights:

**April: Orlando Thomas** *Minnesota Vikings* Arrested and charged with battery against his wife. Avoided jail term after no-contest plea.

**June: Leonard Little** *St. Louis Rams* Pleaded guilty to involuntary manslaughter. Ran a red light and crashed into another car, killing a woman driver in 1998. Suspended for eight games.

**July: Jumbo Elliott, Jason Fabini** *N.Y. Jets*, **Matt O'Dwyer** *Cincinnati Bengals* All arrested after a bar brawl in New York. Elliott, now off the team, pleaded guilty to disorderly conduct and harassment. Fabini's disorderly-conduct charge may be dropped if he says out of trouble for six months. O'Dwyer was sentenced to three years' probation.

**Aug.: Denard Walker** *Tennessee Titans* Pleaded guilty to assault charges filed by his son's mother. Received probation and a two-game suspension.

**Sept.: Peter Warrick** *Florida State, later drafted by Cincinnati Bengals* Arrested with two others on felony grand-theft charges after a shopping-mall episode. Reduced to petty theft. Pleaded no contest.

**Oct.: Steve Muhammad** *Indianapolis Colts* Charged with three counts of misdemeanor battery against his pregnant wife. Pleaded not guilty. Summer trial expected. [Convicted in August 2000.]

**Nov.: Rae Carruth** *Carolina Panthers* Arrested for allegedly plotting the drive-by live in. Until we understand the environments these young men come from, we don't have a clue about the pressures they're under."

Athletes have always been honored as heroes, but in our celebrity-obsessed culture they've reached a whole new level of visibility—especially if they're towering basketball or football players. There's no place to hide, not that they'd want to anyway. "This is a generation of young men who didn't have much growing up," says Harvard University Medical School psychiatry professor Alvin Poussaint. "So when they get something as adults, they wear it on their sleeve so people can be clear they made it. It's important to prove to everyone they've arrived."

And the style of proving it is filtered through the flash and attitude of hip-hop culture. Says NFL superagent Leigh Steinberg: "The rappers want to be ballers and the ballers want to be rappers." Deion Sanders's jewel-bedecked persona made him an original crossover figure, and even now that he's a preacher he's still high-style. "Maybe the guys back in the day didn't wear diamonds and furs, but it's a different day," he says. "I worked for them, I deserve them. I mean, how can you be young with money, good looks and fame and not take advantage of it?"

Such public posturing can be wholly innocent. Regardless, it can attract trouble. NBA star Anthony Mason has had more than his share of nightclub incidents, including a recent assault arrest in New York (he's out on $1,000 bail while the case is still pending). "Everyone's got something to prove," he says. "They think if they prove with you, that gets them a gold star. So you wear a little ice and they think you're flossing, and they start hating you. It's a no-win situation for us." Particularly when the slightest insult can provoke a serious confrontation. "In the hood you don't back down," says University of Southern California assistant professor Todd Boyd. "Any sort of accommodation is considered weakness."

It's even harder to accommodate, of course, when you're traveling in a pack of loyal friends who will do anything to protect your honor. And the athletes protect them back: it's the notion of keeping it real.

shooting that killed pregnant girlfriend. Pleading not guilty to first-degree murder. Awaits trial. [Found not guilty of first degree murder but guilty of conspiracy to commit murder. Sentenced to 20 years in prison.]

**Chris Mims** *San Diego Chargers* Arraigned for four misdemeanors. Charges filed by a man claiming Mims attacked him with a belt at a fastfood chain and stole his tacos. Pleaded guilty to only one: assault with a deadly weapon (his belt).

**Lawrence Taylor** *Ex-N.Y. Giant, Hall of Famer* Pleaded no contest to buying crack cocaine from undercover cop.

**Dec.: Cecil Collins** *Miami Dolphins* Arrested for burglary after allegedly breaking into his neighbor's occupied apartment. Pleaded not guilty. Summer trial expected. [Jailed on a parole violation.]

**Jan.: Rod Smith** *Denver Broncos* Surrendered to police on charges of third-degree assault and harassment involving his wife. Pleaded not guilty. Trial is expected in June. [Pleaded guilty in July 2000; sentenced to probation.]

**Feb.: Fred Lane** *Carolina Panthers* Arrested with three others for allegedly carrying 1.3 grams of marijuana and a .22-caliber rifle. Matter set to go before a grand jury in June. [Shot to death, allegedly by his wife during a domestic dispute, in July 2000.]

**Steve Foley** *Cincinnati Bengals* Charged with battery based on a complaint filed by his son's mother. Pleaded not guilty. Trial is expected to take place this summer. [Cleared in Spring 2000.]

**Sebastian Janikowski** *Florida State, later drafted by Oakland Raiders* Facing bribery charges for allegedly offering $300 to police for the release of roommate in custody. Plea: not guilty. May face deportation.

**Ray Lewis** *Baltimore Ravens* Indicted for murder with two others in the stabbing deaths of two men. Pleaded not guilty. Trial is ongoing. [Pleaded guilty to obstructing justice and avoided jail time.]

**March: Mario Bates** *Arizona Cardinals* Arrested on domestic-violence charges against his girlfriend. Pleaded not guilty.

**April: Todd Marinovich** *Los Angeles Raiders, now in arena football* Arrested based on a woman's claim of rape. Municipal-court arraignment postponed, and formal charges are not yet filed.

**De'Mond Parker** *Green Bay Packers* Charged with marijuana possession; may be dropped upon completion of court-approved drug course.

**May: Dimitrius Underwood** *Dallas Cowboys* Convicted of reckless driving at 95 mph. On appeal.

**Bam Morris, Tamarick Vanover** *Ex-Kansas City Chiefs*. Morris was indicted for drug and money-laundering activities; pleaded not guilty. Vanover pleaded guilty to sale of a stolen vehicle and is cooperating with the investigation.

**Mark Chmura** *Green Bay Packers* Charged with sexual assault against his 17-year-old babysitter who said he had sex with her at a party after a high-school prom. Chmura's lawyer filed a motion to dismiss. [Acquitted in February 2001.]

Source: News reports, research by Sam Register, Kevin Peraino, Fe Conway

Athletes from the poorest neighborhoods once sought to escape their old stomping grounds and every remnant of it. Today's stars fight to remain connected. "Staying true to the hood is extremely important to these young men when they make it," says University of Pennsylvania sociologist Elijah Anderson. "Being considered a sellout is the worst thing imaginable to the hip-hop generation. You may move out, but you can't let go of the hood or of the people who saw you come up. It's the kiss of death for you as a star."

Ray Lewis, as it happens, grew up in a relatively stable environment in Lakeland, Fla. He acquired an entourage only later on. When opening arguments in the trial begin this week, Lewis's defense attorneys will portray him as nothing worse than an unsuccessful peacemaker in a nasty street squabble. The implication will be clear: it was the *other guys* who were fighting, and Lewis is merely guilty of a questionable choice of companions. And they were questionable: one of his codefendants, an aspiring rapper named Reginald Oakley, was charged with some 25 criminal counts between 1985 and 1992; the other, Joe Sweeting, is a convicted felon who also did time in federal prison for a firearms violation.

The notion of a grown man led astray by his companions doesn't provoke a whole lot of sympathy. But Dana London, director of Transition Teams, an education and support group for pro athletes, says the continual demands on athletes from friends comes up more often than any other issue when young athletes talk about off-field problems. "Every friend's got a business idea, every one wants to hang out," she says. "When you're a professional athlete, you can't buy a friend a Civic. They want a BMW, a Lexus." Whatever the athlete's generous intentions, paying all the bills changes the dynamic. "If a person is part of your posse, they evolve from a friend into an employee," says Calvin Hill. Which fuses the friendships with tensions.

But it's only logical that some athletes would want to stick with their old buddies. "What are they going to start doing? Call Donald Trump or Bill Gates and say, 'Let's have a drink'?" adds London.

Indeed, many athletes say their posses get them through. NBA superstar Allen Iverson still rolls with his homeboys—as many as eight, like Iverson, with baggy pants, oversize sweaters and corn-rows—from a rough patch of his hometown of Hampton, Va. He supports them, and most of them bunk at his plush mansion in the Philly suburbs. "These guys are family, like blood to me," he says. "People don't understand how these guys fought for me as a kid. I can't and don't want to send them away just when I get a little success. They're who I am. Dissing them is like dissing me."

NBA Commissioner David Stern insists that "as a rule the posse thing has been a plus for us in the league," and cites Kevin Garnett of the Minnesota Timberwolves. Garnett arrived in Minneapolis right out of high school with his OBF—"Official Block Family"—from back home in Mauldin, S.C. "It's scary, but you can't trust anybody at this level," says the all-star forward. "I need people who knew me when. They keep me grounded."

***Team owners are increasingly distressed by the off-field ugliness, if only because they recognize the bottom-line implications.***

All of this, though, merely widens the cultural chasm between today's stars, so many of them black from impoverished circumstances, and the largely white, upper-middle-class fans who buy tickets. Will they still pay? Team owners are increasingly distressed by the off-field ugliness, if only because they recognize the bottom-line implications. Take the NBA's Charlotte Hornets, which this year had almost as many courtroom as court appearances. Three Hornets were charged with crimes in separate incidents, a fourth was killed in a drag race and a fifth was cited for reckless driving. (Team owner George Shinn was also embroiled in a civil case alleging sexual assault, which he ultimately won.) Amid the distractions the team still made the playoffs, but played at home to a half-filled arena. In Green Bay, where the Packers face a critical vote on a $295 million stadium renovation, public support dropped sharply after Chmura's arrest.

The NFL may not admit to a crisis, but this year it has invested more money and time than ever in screening for prospective draftees, from investigations to psychological testing to one-on-one interviews. The league is also putting a little more sting in its response to off-field misdeeds. For the first time last season the NFL suspended players for off-field criminal activities. While the league conducts a mandatory four-day seminar for all rookies, it is considering requiring special counseling for those with checkered histories.

Programs and seminars are no substitute, however, for a little help from your friends—the right kind of friends. Wide receiver Randy Moss was one of the most talented players in the entire 1998 draft. But by the time he joined the NFL, he already had lost scholarships at Notre Dame and Florida State, served time for assault, had a second jail stint after testing positive for marijuana and had been charged with domestic battery against the mother of his two children. Those charges were eventually dropped, but they cost him millions of dollars when he wasn't drafted until the 21st selection. "You get a lot of attention at a young age, and it can really screw you up," says the Vikings star, who in two seasons has stayed out of trouble and is now the best receiver in the game. "You get into things and you don't know how much they're going to haunt you down the road. It's so easy to get caught up in the moment, and one thing leads to another until you can't stop it. Then you deal with the consequences—and boy do you have to deal with them for a long time."

Moss had someone to lean on. Even before the first training camp, Vikings star receiver Cris Carter, a born-again Christian who says he "dabbled in the gutter," was on the phone to Moss volunteering his services as a mentor. The world of athletic stardom can be as insular as the police force—nobody can understand a cop except another cop. "Cris had been there and knew what it was like to go down the wrong path—way down," says Moss. Carter says he believes the best approach is a buddy system, a one-on-one, athlete-to-athlete approach. "The NFL has done all it can with its programs," he says. "At a certain point, it's on the individuals." Moss agrees. "There are a lot of haters out there who want you to screw up, so you have to check yourself," he says. "But at the end of the day, it's on you if something goes down." That's certainly true. But because they're athletes, it's on the rest of us, too.

# Boxing Reformers Should Go for KO[5]

BY JACK NEWFIELD AND WALLACE MATTHEWS
*NEW YORK POST*, MAY 11, 2000

In bullfighting, it's known as "the moment of truth."

In boxing, it's that point in a fight when one of the fighters is weak and tottering and ready to be taken out.

It's the moment when the crowd is screaming, "Finish him off!" and in that situation, the worst thing a boxer can do is let his cut and fatigued opponent escape the corner.

Right now, the opponent is the parasites who have been preying on boxing. They are ripe to be taken. And the ones to do it are the boxers themselves.

With a federal trial in Newark threatening to topple the corruption-ridden International Boxing Federation, an internal investigation about to turn the New York State Athletic Commission upside down, and a newly released report by state Attorney General Eliot Spitzer detailing how to clean up the fight game, there is no better time for boxing reform than right now.

And everyone, it seems, is jumping onto the pile.

"There are two cancers destroying boxing," said Seth Abraham, the president of Time Warner Sports, boxing's richest and most generous bankroller. "One is the sanctioning bodies, and the other is the rankings within those sanctioning bodies."

On this, the attorney general and the television executive agree.

Clean up the rankings, and you go a long way to cleaning up boxing. Rankings-for-sale are the root of boxing's system that exploits the fighters, politicizes the sport and makes a mockery of the integrity of multimillion-dollar matches.

The Spitzer report's most radical remedy is the creation of an impartial, independent poll of boxing writers and historians to replace the laughable and often corrupt ratings of the existing sanctioning bodies: the IBF, World Boxing Council, World Boxing Association and World Boxing Organization.

And the Abraham proposal takes it a vital step further—the adoption of such a poll by the TV networks to determine title matchups and elimination bouts in place of the capricious and crooked rating systems currently in use.

5. Article by Jack Newfield and Wallace Matthews from *New York Post* May 11, 2000. Copyright © *New York Post*. Reprinted with permission.

Such a move would be the single most purifying act in recent boxing history, since Muhammad Ali beat Sonny Liston for the heavyweight title, liberating it from mob control.

"HBO and Time Warner would enthusiastically support an impartial blue-ribbon poll of writers and historians," Abraham said. "We would use it to make fights. We would recognize them on the air immediately."

But for such a move to work, it would need the support of boxing's most popular and respected champions.

Oscar De La Hoya, Roy Jones Jr., Lennox Lewis all have the power and the opportunity to do for boxing what free-agency pioneer Curt Flood did for baseball.

Any one of them could take a stand—a potentially risky stand—and refuse to be extorted by the alphabet soups.

They could tell the sanctioning bodies what fans already know: that the boxers—not the cheap and gaudy title belts they fight over—are the attraction.

"I have already spoken to the elite champions HBO has under contract, and told them a blue-ribbon panel's ratings would benefit them financially and commercially," Abraham said. "They would no longer have to pay sanction fees out of their pockets to these groups, who are a cancer on boxing."

If Jones or Lewis or De La Hoya said they would base their title defenses solely on an independent poll of writers, the rankings bandits would go out of business overnight.

But the effect would not stop there. Without rankings—and the power to strip champions of their titles—the organizations would no longer be able to appoint inexperienced, unqualified and possibly dishonest judges and referees to work their fights, returning that authority to state commissions.

Spitzer said yesterday he would "do anything I can" to prod the media corporations that broadcast boxing into recognizing the writer's poll instead of the bogus and biased listings of the sanctioning organizations.

Abraham said his powerful corporation would be willing to spearhead such a movement for the survival of the sport—and help raise the money from other corporate sponsors to make it happen.

"The fans don't care about the alphabet organizations," he said. "They recognize champions and want good matchups."

The Spitzer report is a good stiff jab in behalf of reform.

Reports that Tony Russo and James Polsinello, the two worst political hacks on the NYSAC payroll, are about to be canned, are a series of body blows delivered for boxing redemption.

And the creation of an independent panel to provide honest rankings would be the finisher, the punch that sends the parasites to the canvas for good.

The moment to strike is now.

# V. The Business of Sports

Ronald Martinez/Allsport

*Enron Field, home of the Houston Astros, on Opening Day, April 7, 2000. Enron Energy Services has agreed to pay the Astros $100 million over 30 years for the naming rights to the ballpark.*

# *Editor's Introduction*

As fans are reminded whenever their favorite sports teams raise ticket prices, and players demonstrate when they eschew franchise loyalty to sign multimillion-dollar free-agent contracts with former rivals, the business of sports is just that—a business. Indeed, during the 20th century it grew to be one of the biggest businesses in America, earning nearly $400 billion dollars a year by 1999. Despite complaints about high ticket and concession prices and cynicism about greedy owners and players, fans continue to buy team merchandise and attend games in record numbers, thereby helping to make this, as one writer says, a "golden age of sport." Section V explores the variety of ways in which sports teams generate their vast income and the direction in which the sports industry may be headed.

The section opens with Rick Burton's historical look at the business of American sports, "From Hearst to Stern: The Shaping of an Industry over a Century." Beginning with the granting of Major League Baseball's antitrust exemption in 1922, Burton covers several groundbreaking developments, including the NFL's negotiation of a network TV contract during the 1960s; outfielder Curt Flood's challenge of baseball's reserve clause, which paved the way for free agency; and the introduction of ESPN as the first sports entertainment network. Robert Jabaily's article, "Goal Lines, Baselines, and Bottom Lines: Can Pro Sports Survive Prosperity?" focuses on what he calls the "Big Four"—baseball, basketball, football, and hockey—to examine how these sports monopolize industry revenue. While he attributes their success primarily to "a surge in market demand and the market power of the leagues," Jabaily touches on many key issues, including the signing of high-priced players, revenue sharing, suggestions for increasing economic competition among teams, and the financial losses that could result if the distance between players and fans continues to widen. Mark Dolliver considers the plight of the fans as he summarizes a *Sports Illustrated* study about the effects of rising ticket prices on attendance at professional sporting evens in "What Price Victory? Too Much for Some Fans."

For those disgruntled by the power of large-market teams and their seemingly permanent advantage over their poorer rivals, Eric M. Leifer proposes a complete restructuring of the industry in "The Ultimate Expansion." Instead of major league teams affiliating themselves with specific cities, thereby restricting their appeal regionally or locally, Leifer reports that teams may soon be entirely affiliated with corporations, such as Coca-Cola or Nike. Such teams, he explains, would attract the global attention that major league organizations have craved for so many years. As evidence that sports franchises are already experimenting with this type of structure, Leifer points to the fact that they currently sell the naming rights of stadiums and arenas to corporations. This practice is the subject of Filip Bondy's article, "Is It a Stadium or a Commercial?" Although Bondy writes primarily from a sportswriter's point of view, he expresses the confusion felt by many fans who, having attended games in the same building for years, must now call the old stadium or arena by its new corporate name, or whose favorite team has moved to a venue with an impersonal corporate logo attached to it.

The final article in Section V, "Going to Extremes," by Laura Petrecca, looks at the way ESPN's X Games and other extreme sports tournaments are marketed to 12- to 24-year-olds. As Petrecca reports, there is big money in these events, and extreme athletes are becoming celebrities, particularly among teenage boys, their primary audience.

# From Hearst to Stern: The Shaping of an Industry over a Century[1]

BY RICK BURTON
*NEW YORK TIMES*, DECEMBER 19, 1999

The giants of sports are usually celebrated on the fields of play. But in the last century, sports industrialists made decisions that forever changed how American consumers think of sports and shaped an industry that now reaps almost $400 billion annually. Spectator sports, equipment and apparel, licensing, news media investments, sponsorship and stadium construction have evolved significantly from these inspired moments.

What follows is a compendium of the most important developments in sports business. Many of these giants of the boardroom and broadcasting booth are immediately familiar, but some towered only briefly before others modified their actions.

## The Protection of Baseball

The development of baseball in the early 1900's created team sport as a business. Three early landmarks:

- The selection of Kenesaw Mountain Landis, a federal district judge and baseball devotee, to hear a 1915 restraint of trade and antitrust suit between the fledgling Federal League and Major League Baseball. Landis would ultimately note that he was "shocked" that any party would consider "playing baseball 'labor,'" and that baseball must be seen as a "national institution."
- Landis's subsequent selection in 1920 as commissioner of professional baseball, which led to a lifetime ban for eight Chicago White Sox players accused of fixing the 1919 World Series. Landis's "absolute authority" and fervent commitment to keeping baseball pure (and outlawing all gambling associations) became a foundation of American sport.
- In 1922, Supreme Court Justice Oliver Wendell Holmes issued a decision granting Major League Baseball an antitrust exemption. This, despite his observation that while "owners produce baseball games as a source of profit, (they) cannot change the

1. Article by Rick Burton from *New York Times* December 19, 1999. 

character of the games. They are still sport, not trade." This finding would shape all leagues that were to follow.

**Sports Licensing**

The first sports licensing agreement is thought to have taken place in 1928, when David Warsaw persuaded Phil Wrigley to allow Warsaw's company, Sports Specialties, to produce ceramic ashtrays in the shape of Wrigley Field. When Warsaw offered to pay a royalty for every ashtray sold, Wrigley took the deal. Almost 35 years later, Sports Specialties became the National Football League's first licensee.

---

***By the 1920's, broadcasting of sports events on radio established the power of sport as mass entertainment and as a way to sell advertising and radios.***

---

**Newspapers and Radio**

Any review of sport business is incomplete without William Randolph Hearst's 1895 creation of the first sports section for *The New York Journal*. From then on, the importance of sports as media content was clear.

By the 1920's, broadcasting of sports events on radio established the power of sport as mass entertainment and as a way to sell advertising and radios. *Radio Digest* reported that 127 fight fans "dropped dead" while listening to Graham McNamee's dramatic calling of the second Jack Dempsey–Gene Tunney heavyweight fight. McNamee became the first sportscaster celebrity and the first nonathlete sports entertainer.

Corporate America's realization that sport worked efficiently was evident when Ford Motor Company committed more than $100,000 to sponsor the 1934 World Series on multiple radio networks. The televising of sports began in 1939.

**The N.F.L. and Television**

While much more credit is generally (and deservedly) given to Pete Rozelle, it was an earlier N.F.L. commissioner, Bert Bell, who gave permission for television timeouts in 1958 to increase advertising access and revenue. That same year, Bell watched the Baltimore Colts beat the New York Giants in sudden death and realized football's enormous national appeal to television.

By the time Rozelle took over in 1960, it was clear that the N.F.L. could use television for great gains in national popularity. Rozelle's creation of the marketing arm NFL Properties in 1963 and his $28.2 million television contract with CBS in 1964 initiated new ways to view leagues as business portfolios. His 1970 go-ahead for ABC's *Monday Night Football* (working with ABC's Roone Arledge, a pioneer of sports TV) opened the door to regularly scheduled prime time sports.

### Palmer's Agent

While the representation of athletes had been around for more than 60 years (recognizing particularly Madison Square Garden's Tex Rickard), Mark McCormack's 1960 decision to leave a Cleveland law firm and represent Arnold Palmer was a landmark move. It firmed up the concept of athlete as revenue generator through endorsements, appearances and product sponsorship. McCormack's further development of International Management Group as an event promoter-producer and TV show syndicator changed "the art of the deal" dramatically.

### The Astrodome

Originally billed the Eighth Wonder of the World by the Houston Astros' er, Judge Roy Hofheinz, the Astrodome was unveiled in 1965 and forever changed the way outdoor sports were presented. Hofheinz coined the phrase "sky boxes" for his luxury suites and then introduced AstroTurf in 1966 when the dome's original natural grass died.

A second key development involving luxury boxes took place in 1988, when the Detroit Pistons' owner, William Davidson, built the Palace at Auburn Hills and designed an indoor arena with 180 luxury suites. The suites essentially financed the construction of his facility. More than 130 stadiums have since been built or renovated in the United States.

### Nike

Gillette, Wheaties and Miller Lite had used sports themes in their advertising, but Nike put sports, marketing, business and pop culture together in a new and dynamic way. Phil Knight, who founded Blue Ribbon Sports, the forerunner of Nike, in 1963, looked at his product as more than just track shoes or basketball shoes, and brilliant ad campaigns with John McEnroe, Michael Jordan, Bo Jackson and Tiger Woods followed.

### Flood's Challenge

After the 1969 season, the St. Louis Cardinals decided they would trade outfielder Curt Flood to Philadelphia. Flood asked Commissioner Bowie Kuhn to "nullify the trade." Kuhn would not, and Flood pursued legal action all the way to the Supreme Court.

In June 1972 the court stayed true to Justice Holmes's earlier decision and denied Flood's request for relief or freedom from the reserve clause, under which baseball teams "owned" their players. But after the 1975 season, pitchers Andy Messersmith and Dave McNally (with the players union leader, Marvin Miller, working behind the scenes) were able to benefit from Flood's one-man revolution. Using the platform Flood had created for challenging the system, both claimed they had "played out their option year" and were free to sell themselves to the highest bidder.

### Title IX

This 1972 action by the federal government mandated equal opportunities for many people in many situations. It is perhaps best known because it demands equal athletic scholarship opportunities for women attending institutions receiving federal support.

While some National Collegiate Athletic Association schools are still not in compliance 27 years later, the effects of Title IX were most obvious last summer when the United States Women's World Cup soccer team articulated Girl Power across America.

### ESPN

Bill Rasmussen, a sportscaster for an NBC affiliate in Springfield, Mass., determined in 1978 that an all-sports cable network was logical. Rasmussen's Entertainment and Sports Programming Network was started on Sept. 7, 1979, with George Grande and Lee Leonard as hosts of the first *SportsCenter*. On Sept. 20 that year, RCA awarded ESPN satellite positions, leading to 24-hour sports programming.

### Stern's Innovations

Two decisive moves in 1999 by David Stern, the National Basketball Association commissioner, will have tremendous impact on the future of sport. With his creation of *NBA.com* TV, the N.B.A. became the first professional sports league to establish its own cable/satellite television network and at the same time offered the hope of interactive programming down the road. With his resolution of the 1998–99 lockout, Stern capped player capitalism and brought financial certainty to basketball, the professional team sport featuring the highest average ticket prices. In both, Stern influenced professional sports' spiraling costs and prepared to embrace the computer's interactive flexibility.

# Goal Lines, Baselines, and Bottom Lines: Can Pro Sports Survive Prosperity?[2]

BY ROBERT JABAILY
*FEDERAL RESERVE BANK OF BOSTON REGIONAL REVIEW, Q3,* 1999

If ever there was a "Golden Age of Sport," this could be it. Business is booming, and the quality of play is as good, or better, than ever.

Nostalgia buffs might try to tell you that no one will ever top Babe Ruth and the '27 Yankees or Bill Russell and the old Celtics or . . . fill in the blank. But the fact is that Michael Jordan and Mark McGwire match up very well against the heroes of yesteryear. You could, as Casey used to say, look it up.

The dollars and cents look good, too. Attendance is up, TV viewership is strong, franchises in major markets cost almost as much as the Manhattan Project, and superstar salaries sometimes exceed the GDP of a small country.

Yet, during the 1980s and 1990s, each of the "Big Four"—Major League Baseball, the NBA, the NFL, and the NHL—flirted with killing the golden goose. A succession of player strikes and owner lockouts cost both sides hundreds of millions of dollars in lost salaries and revenues—not to mention the incalculable loss of fan goodwill. And if the owner/player death dance isn't enough to alienate fans, there is growing internal tension in all four leagues that pits owner against owner and player against player.

Meanwhile, fans just shake their heads and wonder why the millionaires and billionaires can't find a way to share the wealth.

## Power Play

Two factors, in combination, are largely responsible for the enormous prosperity of big-time pro sports: a surge in demand and the market power of the leagues.

The "Big Four" are not actual monopolies. In fact, only Major League Baseball is exempt from federal antitrust laws. But the NBA, NFL, NHL, and MLB are able to generate tremendous revenues by using their market power to limit economic competition.

---

2. Article by Robert Jaabaily from *Federal Reserve Bank of Boston Regional Review, Q3,* 1999. 

For starters, leagues restrict the overall number of franchises and guarantee each team a territorial monopoly. League approval and a steep franchise fee stand in the way of prospective new team owners, and leagues even have the power to block an owner from moving an existing team to a new city. (Unless, of course, the owner is Al Davis, who successfully sued the NFL when it tried to stop him from moving his Oakland Raiders to Los Angeles in 1979.)

Launching a new league is an option for anyone determined to own a pro sports team, but going head to head against the "Big Four" is no easy task. The one truly successful new league in modern sports history was the American Football League, and its survival proved the old adage that "timing is everything." Conditions for starting a new pro football league were ideal in 1960: Fans were going wild for the game, the relationship between sports and television was beginning to flourish, and the NFL had been slow to expand into new markets.

***Because of their market power, sports leagues are well positioned to maximize revenue.***

But more often than not, new leagues fail. The American Basketball Association, the American Basketball League, and the World Hockey Association lasted only a few seasons. The United Baseball League never even made it to opening day. Lack of TV revenue and the competition for high-priced talent sealed their fate.

**Winner Take All**

Because of their market power, sports leagues are well positioned to maximize revenue. Whether they're bargaining with local politicians or TV executives, the "Big Four" often enjoy a tremendous edge.

If, for example, a team is angling for taxpayers to pick up the cost of a new stadium, the league's de facto monopoly provides considerable leverage. "In real life, the threat is, 'Build it or we will leave,'" writes *Washington Post* sports columnist Thomas Boswell. And although he is talking about baseball, Boswell's observation applies just as easily to other pro sports.

Leagues have also learned how to get the most out of television networks. The TV sports gold rush began in 1964, when Commissioner Pete Rozelle convinced NFL team owners to let the league negotiate a joint television agreement on their behalf. (Rozelle's initiative followed a 1962 Congressional antitrust exemption for league television contracts.) The NFL's first national TV contract—

a two-year, $28 million deal with CBS—seemed like a fortune at the time. But by 1998, the NFL had TV agreements with the four networks totaling $17.6 billion over eight years.

Licensed products—caps, shirts, cards, computer games, toys, snackfood, beverages, anything with a sports logo on it—are another rich source of revenue that experienced spectacular growth when the "Big Four" established league-wide marketing and merchandising units. NBA Commissioner David Stern pioneered the concept, but everyone else caught on fast. By the end of the 1990s, pro football led the pack with retail sales of NFL-licensed goods totaling $3.6 billion.

Business is brisk at the box office, too. NBA per-game attendance has increased by more than 70 percent since 1980, while the NFL has been at 95 percent of capacity for years. And if the 1994–95 strike did any lasting damage to Major League Baseball, you couldn't prove it by looking at the Cleveland market, where a new ballpark helped the Indians to sell out every seat for the entire 1996 season—before opening day.

No wonder average ticket prices for all four leagues have climbed by at least 70 percent since 1991. NFL tickets have increased the most—83 percent, from $25.21 in 1991 to $38.09 in 1998—but NHL tickets are the priciest—$40.64 during the 1998-99 season. And those are average prices. Let's not even talk about filmmaker

## The Revenue Gap

Baseball owners claim that the widening revenue gap between prosperous and struggling teams will undermine competitive balance and reduce revenues and franchise values—especially in markets where fans know the home team doesn't have a prayer of reaching the playoffs. The owners would solve this problem by capping salaries; the players say let the rich owners share their revenues with the poor, as they do in the NFL.

| | Highest Revenue Team | | Lowest Revenue Team | | Ratio |
|---|---|---|---|---|---|
| MLB | N.Y. Yankees | $144.7 | Montreal Expos | $43.6 | 3.3x1 |
| NHL* | Detroit Red Wings | 80.1 | Carolina Hurricanes | 25.1 | 3.2x1 |
| NBA* | Chicago Bulls | 112.2 | Denver Nuggets | 37.8 | 3.0x1 |
| NFL** | Dallas Cowboys | 118.0 | Jacksonville Jaguars | 66.8 | 1.8x1 |

Note: Revenues in millions. *Figures are for 1997–98. **Figures are for 1997.
Source: *Forbes,* December 14, 1998

Spike Lee's $1,350-per-game courtside seats for Knicks games at Madison Square Garden, or NFL luxury suites that cost as much as $350,000 per season in 1998.

Rising revenues from TV, licensed goods, and gate receipts have meant flush times for players, too. Free agency gave them the power to channel a greater share of sports revenues from the owners' pockets to their own, and they are now able to command salaries that are more in line with their market value. Average salaries in all four leagues top $1 million, and superstar earnings are in the stratosphere. Michael Jordan, the best paid athlete in 1997, earned $31 million in salary and $47 million in endorsements.

Yes, that's a lot of money for playing a game, but superstars earn as much as they do because they generate phenomenal revenue for their teams. They are marquee players who capture fans' hearts—and entertainment dollars—through a combination of exceptional talent and "star power." Without them, pro sports would be less exciting and less lucrative.

***Revenues matter because wealthy teams almost always win the competition to attract and keep top talent.***

Owners may fret over the high cost of attracting and keeping top talent, but the fact is that they are parting with their money willingly—if not always cheerfully or wisely—and they rarely pay more than they expect a superstar to generate in revenue. In a sense, superstar salaries are a measure of sports prosperity.

### Rich versus Super Rich

So, if times are so good, why is the modern sports scene so contentious? Economists James Quirk and Rodney Fort believe the market power of leagues is to blame. The authors of *Pay Dirt* and *Hard Ball* argue that the leagues' monopoly profits have become "the prize package" at the center of most disputes.

Squabbling between owners and players makes most of the headlines, but as often as not the main event is really between owners—with side action between superstars and middle-class players becoming more of a factor every season. The dynamic varies from sport to sport, as does the outcome, but disagreements over the division of wealth are always the center of controversy.

Major League Baseball, for example, is thriving, but a growing revenue imbalance between markets is threatening the game's overall prosperity and popularity. *Forbes* magazine estimated that the wealthy New York Yankees earned total revenues of $144.7 million for the 1997 season, while the perennially strapped Montreal Expos

> Since free agency, players have managed to capture an increasing percentage of league revenues—prompting team owners to fight back with salary caps and even lockouts.
>
> **ITEM:** More than 127.5 million American television viewers sat around the national campfire to watch the 1999 Super Bowl. Advertisers paid an average of $1.6 million for 30 seconds of commercial time during the broadcast.
>
> **ITEM:** Michael Jordan topped the 1999 *Forbes* Power 100 list, which measures a combination of "income and media buzz." Oprah placed second; former President George Bush rounded out the field at number 100.
>
> **ITEM:** After the 1998 season, pitcher Kevin Brown left the San Diego Padres to sign a seven-year, $105 million contract with the Los Angeles Dodgers. If the 33-year-old Brown averages 15 wins per season over the next seven years—no sure thing—the Dodgers will have paid him $1 million per victory.
>
> **ITEM:** In early 1999, a Maryland businessman and a New York City banker offered $800 million for the NFL's Washington Redskins franchise.

earned $43.6 million. The gap in 1997 media revenues was equally striking—$69.8 million for the Yankees versus $18.5 million for the Expos.

Revenues matter because wealthy teams almost always win the competition to attract and keep top talent. The Yankees' star outfielder Bernie Williams earned $8.3 million for 1998—an amount equal to the Expos' entire 1998 payroll. The Yankees also won the 1998 World Series, while the Expos barely managed to stay out of the cellar in the National League East.

Baseball owners worry that the widening gaps in revenue and payroll will erode competitive balance on the field and create a permanent split between "have" and "have not" teams. They are concerned that the overall entertainment value of their product will suffer, especially in markets where fans know the home team is out of the running before the season opens.

In the owners' collective nightmare, the same wealthy teams go to the playoffs every season, and fans begin to lose interest—even in prosperous markets—because a steady diet of wins can be almost as tedious as an endless string of losses. Ticket sales and TV ratings sag, revenues drop, and franchise values weaken.

It's a sobering prospect, but players don't buy it. The way they see it, owners are using competitive balance as an excuse to recapture revenues at the players' expense. When owners claim financial difficulty, players raise their eyebrows and ask to see the teams' financial records. Most teams, however, are privately held rather than publicly traded, which means owners are under no obligation to share their financials with anyone. So the books remain closed and players' skepticism deepens.

The long history of mutual distrust between owners and players, coupled with the owners' rising anxiety over revenues, salaries, and competitive balance, made the 1994–95 baseball strike almost inevitable. The real conflict, however, was a behind-the-scenes struggle between owners who lacked a strong common interest and a unified strategy for addressing their concerns. All the owners—rich and poor—agreed on the easy stuff. Their clear preference was to control labor costs and restore competitive balance by capping salaries, but for obvious reasons players were dead set against the idea.

Another option would have been for prosperous franchises to share some of their wealth with struggling teams, but rich owners were unwilling to part with more than a fraction of their revenues. So finally, unable to agree on any other strategy, MLB team owners decided to pick a fight with the players union. Their ultimate objective was to recapture revenue by forcing players to accept a salary cap, but the players refused to buckle. In the end, the players union was able to outlast the owners by convincing its members that they had compelling economic reasons for sticking together. The strike ended when a relatively small but influential group of owners pressed for a settlement after deciding that the battle for a salary cap was costing them more than they could possibly hope to gain.

The 1998–99 NBA lockout had similar origins but a very different outcome. At the heart of the dispute, wrote David Warsh of the *Boston Globe*, was the "inability to share out $2 billion in overall NBA revenues among 29 owners and 400 players." When the lockout began, 57 percent of the league's revenues were going to the players; owners wanted to roll that figure back to 53 percent. The lockout ended after both sides agreed to split the difference and settled on 55 percent.

NBA owners, executives, and players thought they had found a formula for fiscal sanity and labor peace when they originated the salary cap concept in 1984. But by the late 1990s, the cap had lost much of its effectiveness, largely because the so-called "Larry Bird exception" allowed teams to re-sign their own players at any price. As superstar salaries climbed, the "Bird" exception undermined the cap to the point where the Chicago Bulls were able to exclude Michael Jordan's $31 million paycheck from their 1997–98 ceiling. On top of that, the annual team cap had mushroomed from $3.6 million in 1984 to $24 million in 1996.

By the end of the 1997–98 season NBA owners were ready to try something drastic. In an effort to reclaim a "fair share of the revenues," they voted to lock players out of training camps and went so far as to set a deadline for canceling the entire season.

The owners prevailed, in part because they were willing to throw their undivided support behind NBA Commissioner David Stern, but also because the basketball players union was unable to convince its members that outlasting the owners was worth losing an entire season's paycheck. Much of the pressure to reach a settlement came from middle-class players and rookies who were beginning to wonder why they should endure the economic impact of a lockout when the issues at stake mainly affected the earnings of superstars.

***The NFL has been the most successful at sharing the wealth and smoothing out the imbalance between markets.***

**Winner Share**

The NFL has been the most successful at sharing the wealth and smoothing out the imbalance between markets. Its history of cooperative action dates back to the early 1960s, when team owners agreed to give NFL Commissioner Pete Rozelle enough authority to convince, cajole, and coerce individual franchises into cooperating for the common good. Today, television and licensing revenues are shared equally, and gate receipts are shared generously, 60 percent for the home team and 40 percent for the visitors. The league also has maximum and minimum team payroll limits—no more than $64.3 million and no less than $55 million during the 1998–99 season.

The results of the NFL's cooperative approach are plain to see. Pro football tops all other sports in the revenues it generates from TV agreements and the sale of licensed merchandise, and the gap between its richest and poorest teams is by far the narrowest of all four leagues. NFL franchises thrive in small markets such as Green Bay, Wisconsin (pop. 102,000+), and in otherwise marginal markets such as Pittsburgh, where professional baseball and hockey teams are barely hanging on and the NBA doesn't even have a presence. According to a 1998 Harris Poll in *USA Today,* 28 percent of adult Americans rank pro football as their favorite sport —baseball finished second with 17 percent, and basketball came in third with 13 percent. Pro football's popularity and prosperity reflect the fact that NFL owners and executives have managed to create a truly national market for their game. Fans who ordinarily just follow the hometown team in other sports, regularly tune to *Monday Night Football* regardless of who the featured teams are.

But even in the NFL, owners' interests are diverging and cooperation is beginning to break down. Newer owners, who paid top dollar for their franchises during the 1990s and borrowed heavily to finance their purchases, are chafing under the old share-and-share-alike arrangement. Some are pressing to keep a larger share of the revenue their teams generate. And at least one, Dallas Cowboys owner Jerry Jones, has made separate advertising and licensing deals with competitors of official NFL sponsors and licensees. None of this sits well with league officials and longtime owners, who have prospered under the revenue-sharing arrangement.

The feud has been marked by lawsuits and a rising level of personal acrimony. Whether the tensions will degenerate into all-out war between the old order and the new is anyone's guess.

**Regulation Time**

James Quirk and Rodney Fort have a proposal for revamping the business of pro sports. They think the time has come to try something revolutionary—true business competition.

Quirk and Fort contend that "essentially all of the many problems of the pro team sports business arise from one simple fact, namely the monopoly power of pro team sports leagues. . . . Eliminate that monopoly power and you eliminate almost every one of the problems of the sports business."

The core of their proposal calls for a Justice Department antitrust action to break up each of the existing leagues—MLB, the NBA, the NFL, and the NHL—into four independent leagues, each with roughly eight teams. The leagues would compete against one another for everything—players, TV contracts, franchise locations, and fans. There would be no more territorial monopolies; so, in theory, any city that could support a team would have one, and the most lucrative markets would attract a cluster of competing teams. A very limited antitrust exemption would permit the competing leagues to coordinate post-season playoffs and championships.

Quirk and Fort believe that the introduction of market forces would narrow the difference between "have" and "have not" teams by reducing the revenue imbalance among league cities. Three or four teams competing for TV revenues and gate receipts in the New York market would make the "Big Apple" more like the "Twin Cities" in terms of each team's revenue potential; and as the revenue gap narrowed, so would the payroll gap. Quirk and Fort also argue that cities would feel less pressure to provide stadium subsidies, because if an existing team threatened to move, another would be free to come and take its place.

At bottom, say Quirk and Fort, eliminating sports monopolies will shift power "from the insiders—owners and players—to the rest of us—fans and taxpayers." If team owners and general managers are compelled to make decisions in a competitive market environment, fans will reap the benefits.

The argument is powerful—in terms of economic theory, public policy, and popular appeal. Introducing more economic competition to the pro sports business would almost certainly diminish the market power of sports leagues and return a measure of control to fans and local officials.

But don't expect greater business competition to be a cure-all. The appeal of pro sports often hinges on a mix of intangibles, and teams like the Cubs, the Red Sox, the Redskins, the Knicks, and the Canadiens have a hold over fans that might make them almost immune to competition. Sure, we are drawn to sports because we enjoy watching the world's best athletes match skills, but we also go to games looking for links to our own past and to the distant past. To some of us, there will never be a team like the one we grew up with, regardless of where we move to and despite the fact that highly paid hired guns now wear the uniforms. It's an emotional attachment that a new team in town might be hard-pressed to compete against.

***There seems to be a growing distance—emotional and financial—between fans and their "heroes."***

Nor will increased business competition guarantee that pro sports will be less fractious. Owners and players have argued over money since the days of high-wheeled bicycles and handlebar mustaches, when the main bones of contention were health insurance, pension plans, and $1,000 raises. Splitting the loot has always been a source of conflict in pro sports and that isn't likely to change—regardless of how much loot there is to split. Sometimes, fighting over money can be a sport in itself.

### All in the Game

Until now, pro sports have been remarkably resilient. Fans have come back after every strike or lockout.

But each dispute has taken its toll. You can hear it in the voices of fans who call the all-sports talk radio stations. Some are angry; others are disenchanted. Many are bewildered.

There seems to be a growing distance—emotional and financial—between fans and their "heroes." Players used to work during the off-season to make ends meet. And not so long ago, even big stars lived in the same neighborhoods as their fans. Sometimes, they even played stickball or shot baskets with the neighborhood kids. But those days are gone, and they are never coming back.

Perhaps the biggest threat to big-time pro sports is that fans, especially young fans, have been finding new outlets for their entertainment dollars: the Internet, the movies, and popular music. In fact, the day might be coming when baseball, basketball, football, and hockey won't even dominate the sports sector of the entertainment market. Fans are increasingly attracted to pro wrestling, NASCAR, soccer, and the X-Games—in large part because the stars of those sports seem more accessible.

Yet, despite all the changes, people keep going to ballgames or following the action on TV, because when all is said and done, sports reward fans by giving them whatever they seek. Those who look for greed, selfishness, and meanness will find all three in abundance. But if they are lucky, they might also experience something to talk about till the end of their days—the sight of Bobby Orr soaring three feet above the ice after his "flying" goal wins the 1970 Stanley Cup, or the everyday beauty of Junior Griffey's smooth, sweet swing.

And even if nothing memorable happens on the field, or on the court, or on the ice, our games still offer us the chance to pass a few pleasant hours in the company of people we enjoy, or the opportunity to savor a season like the summer of 1998 when everyone wanted to know if Mark or Sammy had "hit one today."

# What Price Victory? Too Much for Most Fans[3]

BY MARK DOLLIVER
*ADWEEK*, MAY 22, 2000

Take me out to the ballgame? Only if you're buying the tickets. A survey commissioned by *Sports Illustrated* finds the soaring cost of attending games is estranging people from pro sports. As the chart indicates, the "total cost" is the main factor keeping fans away. With ticket prices having risen four times faster than the Consumer Price Index since 1991, "attending sports events went from being affordable family entertainment to being a corporate perk." Meanwhile, seats sold to those corporate customers often go empty. "Unless it's a playoff game or a particularly compelling regular-season matchup," notes *SI*, "season-ticket holders increasingly just aren't bothering to come." Still, plenty of fans would attend more games if it weren't so pricey. With all due respect to big-screen TVs, 66 percent would like to see a baseball game live, versus 24 percent preferring to watch on the tube. For NBA games, the split was 48 percent "in person" versus 36 percent "on TV"; for hockey, 46 percent "in person" versus 23 percent "on TV." Only for NFL football did "on TV" (48 percent) tally more votes than "in person" (46 percent).

**I'm less likely to attend a sporting event today because of . . .**

| | |
|---|---|
| Total cost to attend | 57% |
| Comfort of watching at home | 41% |
| Players' behavior during games | 41% |
| Traffic and parking | 38% |
| Increase in sports on TV | 35% |
| Lateness of games | 26% |
| TV replay and analysis | 22% |
| Unlikelihood of getting good seats | 19% |
| Change in how local team is doing | 14% |
| Change in family's interest in game | 13% |

3. Article by Mark Dolliver from *Adweek*, May 22, 2000. 

# The Ultimate Expansion[4]

BY ERIC M. LEIFER
*ACROSS THE BOARD*, JUNE 1999

Major-league sports are on the verge of a fundamental reorganization. Like changes of the past, the overhaul will be spurred by the opportunity to expand the audience for sports. Over the last two decades, every sport has looked overseas for growth opportunities. All have established international divisions with foreign offices and hundreds of employees. The lure of international publics will bring pressures for change that will dwarf those once brought by the prospect of local and national publics.

The attachment of teams to cities was once the big leagues' greatest asset. Teams took on the names of host cities and played half of their games at home in exchange for a city's loyal support through the ups and downs of a pennant race. Since support for winning teams is rarely problematic, the viability of early leagues rested on the willingness of host cities to loyally support losing teams. So strong was the attachment between teams and cities in Major League Baseball that not a single team either perished or relocated from 1903 to 1953.

But major leagues have never enjoyed the isolation necessary to be complacent. Attachments to cities and network television have led civic leaders and television executives to meddle in major-league affairs. Large corporations like Nike and Gillette have become highly dependent on major-league sports as advertising vehicles for reaching desired markets.

The rise of network television in the 1950s created new opportunities for the big leagues. It allowed teams to pursue national rather than only local audiences and allowed city residents to follow teams of other cities. The economics of television broadcasting put a huge premium on this kind of disloyalty. For almost 30 years, *Monday Night Football*—one of the most successful ventures in network and league history—has broadcast weekly the trysts of teams from two cities for the pleasure of viewers all over the nation. By actively cultivating such disloyalty, national broadcasters brought in revenues that far exceeded local box receipts.

4. Article by Eric M. Leifer from *Across the Board* June 1999. 

The attachment between teams and cities was weakened by television but not replaced. Fans loyally rooted for their home teams at stadiums, and quietly followed other teams in the privacy of their own homes. Big leagues used the weakened attachment to enlarge their television audiences. Local teams helped recruit new enthusiasts for leaguewide competition on television. To extend geographic coverage, teams were relocated or newly formed and sent into uncharted territories as missionaries for their league. National audiences were built up in part from the local exertions of city teams.

In the process of spanning the nation with local teams, however, big leagues have grown unwieldy in size. Playing talent and broadcast revenues are being spread across too many weak teams. The idea of further expanding the big leagues by placing local teams overseas is unworkable. If anything, the size of global leagues must be smaller in order to involve an unsophisticated international public. Renegade efforts to launch global leagues with city teams, dating back to the 1960s, have never survived even a season. The NFL's World League, a minor league with a spring schedule, struggled for two years with teams in the United States and Europe before retrenching into only European cities.

***Major-league teams are on the verge of reattaching themselves to a new kind of entity—one not rooted in locales.***

## Going, Going . . . Global

Major-league teams are on the verge of reattaching themselves to a new kind of entity—one not rooted in locales. The time has come to recognize that major leagues have outgrown their original format. Local loyalties have become a hindrance to the cultivation of broader publics. Although people may see themselves as loyal fans, the quiet disloyalty of their willingness to watch games between remote teams accounts for 70 percent of NFL revenues. As teams head out to cultivate worldwide fans, there is no way they will also be able to cater to a local public—no matter how largely this is defined. Teams must detach from locales altogether and set out to captivate viewers on an international scale.

The big leagues find themselves caught in a dilemma. In trying to preserve the attachment of teams to cities for domestic audiences, they can offer only peripheral games for overseas audiences. They send players to appear in international events and stage exhibition games abroad, complete with fireworks and rock bands. They broadcast championship games throughout the world and license so much logoed apparel that one German youth thought the NFL was a clothing manufacturer!

The attachment of teams to cities is a liability for global expansion. With no room for overseas-based teams in the big leagues, global audiences cannot have the same basis for identifying with teams as do U.S. audiences. Imagine trying to involve U.S. audiences in an ongoing rivalry between teams attached to Nagoya and Sapporo. In the same vein, why would residents of these Japanese cities follow a rivalry between teams attached to Denver and Kansas City? Furthermore, playing half of one's games in a single location (and the rest in other league locations) is unduly constraining in the quest for global coverage. Big-league teams must be able to move throughout the world in order to stir up local interest in the television broadcasts that will follow them.

Multinational corporations are ideal for the purpose of reattachment, and in many ways, they stand in need of clear identities much as cities and networks once did. These sprawling entities, with hundreds of products and operations spanning scores of countries, are exceedingly hard to conceptualize and hence are vulnerable to the projections of others. Were big-league teams to attach themselves in name to multinationals, they would confer identities to these corporations and provide them some security.

In both football and basketball, attaching teams to corporations has been tried before. Local companies once used this sponsorship to strengthen their ties to the community on which they depended, and professional athletes gained access to managerial careers upon retirement from sports. Today, however, multinational corporations do not depend on the local market, and sports celebrities are hardly motivated by the promise of managerial careers. The attachment of major-league teams to multinationals would serve an altogether different purpose. The international presence of multinationals would give teams both the ability and the need to have an international identity. A Japanese league trying to enter the United States would have an easier time if its teams were attached in name to companies like Sony or Honda than to cities like Nagoya and Sapporo. Conversely, the names of McDonald's or Coca-Cola would arouse more passions in mainland China than would Denver or Kansas City. Rivalries in the global marketplace could spill over into the field of sporting competition. Even the American public might get more enthused over a gridiron showdown between Coke and Pepsi than one between Denver and Atlanta.

As strange as this new attachment might sound, it is already in the making. In 1993, the NHL created a franchise and sold it to Walt Disney & Co., which named the team the Mighty Ducks, after the eponymous 1992 Disney movie. The company followed the film with two sequels, *D2: The Mighty Ducks* in 1994 and *D3: The Mighty Ducks* in 1996. Even people who have heard of the Mighty Ducks team may be unaware that they are based in Anaheim, where they must play half their games. On the other hand, both the team name and this open act of cross-promotion have the effect of attaching the Mighty Ducks to Disney. Should the Ducks ever be freed by the NHL to go out and build an international following, they would do well to call themselves the Disney Mighty Ducks rather than the Anaheim Mighty Ducks.

### Portable Home Teams

Having no locale is a key virtue for multinationals. Big-league teams attached to multinationals would no longer have home locations and, hence, would be free to mobilize support internationally through live appearances. One could easily imagine many sets of teams passing through the same locations, much as teams pass through on the TV screen. Both live and broadcast competition would then be able to involve people in leaguewide competition. Today, the only place local enthusiasts can welcome another pair of city teams into their city is on television. With teams attached to multinationals, there would be no automatic basis for a city to favor a single team, and therefore many teams could be welcomed in live appearances. Teams would be freed of home locations, and home crowds would be freed of seeing the league entirely through the lens of a single team.

The rewards of having international audiences are too great for teams to continue settling in a single place. Movement around the globe would aim to keep people in specific places involved in league competition as a whole and, hence, stimulate widespread interest in television broadcasts. The teams of an entire league might compete in Asia, in Europe, then in North and South America. Seasons could be segmented by these regional movements, with regional champions assured a place in the final season championships alongside overall division champions. This sort of wandering season would allow regional favorites to emerge each year and heighten international interest in the playoffs as each region tuned in to support its favorite team.

Ideally, the current seasons of each big-league sport would be preserved, if only as a way to avoid direct competition between sports. In a global itinerary, however, this would require a year-long season, since seasons vary across hemispheres at any given time. Movement across world regions could loosely follow the movement of seasons so live games could be played in the same season throughout the year. Different sports would continue to have staggered season-starting dates, so that for the American public, the season of live competition would not differ significantly. Different sports, at different stages of their respective seasons, would compete directly only in their televised form. Only one sport at a time would be engaged in post-season playoffs and championship series, given the staggering of season starting dates.

Teams would play wherever stadiums are built and enthusiasts turn out. Stadium construction in the past has been entirely rooted in the attachment of teams to cities. Whether stadiums are financed by team owners or by municipalities, the investment is predicated on the fact that a team will play half of its games in the stadium. This security will be lost as teams detach from cities. Cities will no longer compete over securing a single franchise but will, instead, compete to book individual games among all the teams in a league. In this respect, both risk and opportunities increase for stadium owners. It is likely that multisport stadiums will be constructed in many new locations, possibly as part of entertainment and shopping villages, and will compete year-round for games in all big-league sports.

***Teams would play wherever stadiums are built and enthusiasts turn out.***

**An Unraveling System**

The transition into this strange new world is likely to be triggered, at least in pretext, by conflicts between publicly owned stadiums and team owners. In what has become routine, the owner of a popular team will demand renovations, luxury boxes, or perhaps a new stadium and the city will not comply. The owner will then carry out the standard threat to abandon the stadium, only this time it will not be clear where the owner is planning to take the team. In addition to rescheduling "home" games in other big-league stadiums, some games will be played abroad. After more time has passed and more angry words are exchanged, the new road team will carry out its final threat and drop the city from its name in favor of a corporate attachment.

Meanwhile, the original stadium managers may have succeeded in scheduling the games of other big-league teams who are up to the same antics. This loss will, of course, create a new vacancy that may tempt other teams to abandon their home locations. In short order, city residents may find that they have fewer games to attend (because games played abroad will be lost to the system) but a greater diversity of newly christened corporate teams seeking their support at the box office.

Once the system starts to unravel, it could take only a few seasons for a new prototype to emerge. Although at first the league office might distance itself from the process, it will start to exploit the chaotic situation by pressing for major rule changes that would never be pushed through in normal times. In the end, the league will rename itself to acknowledge the new global scale.

It could be that one day the big leagues will look back with shame over how competition is organized today. Case in point: *The Official NFL Encyclopedia* currently omits all record of the NFL's first 25 years of existence. By current standards, those years are uncomfortably ragged. Teams played for some now-forgotten cities. Instead of playing half of their games at home and half away, they played wherever the largest paying crowd was expected to show up. Losing teams routinely perished, many well before a season ended. Yet for those who followed the NFL in the 1920s and 1930s, there must have been a good deal of pride in the accomplishments of the league, both in terms of its great players and teams and the scale of its finances.

What is now a source of pride may also become an embarrassment in light of what will follow. The basic product of the big leagues—the pennant race between teams attached to cities—is not well designed for global distribution. Under mounting strain, this local 19th-century product may soon have to be radically modified for the global 21st century. The hard-fought pennant races that currently involve us so deeply someday might be quietly dropped from the official record as an embarrassment. Perhaps instead of the record, some myth will be constructed about how the future teams came into being. Perhaps Disney is already in the process of doing this for its Mighty Ducks: In the first movie, Disney's ugly ducklings were transformed by playing ice hockey for the glory of a law firm headed by a Mr. Ducksworth, and not for a locale. Instead of painfully evolving for more than a century, future corporate teams appear destined to mythically rise quickly from humble origins with a few gimmicks and help from lawyers.

No aspect of this strange new world will be brought about easily. More resistance is likely to be met on the home front than abroad. In the United States, change will be construed as a threat rather than an opportunity. Despite the decreasing dependence of teams on local support, the attachment of teams to cities has become too much a part of the natural order of things to be easily abandoned. Yet nearly everything that appears natural today would have seemed quite strange from the standpoint of earlier times, and the strange new world ahead, if it can be brought about, will quickly become the only one that makes sense.

## Buying the Rooting Section

A world filled with corporate-named teams may not have blossomed yet, but the seeds are already planted—Walt Disney & Co., for instance, owns a major-league team (see main story). Corporations have always influenced sports through advertising, of course, but "promotional considerations" are taking on new meanings. In many cities, corporations own, sponsor, or purchase naming rights to stadiums. Whoever said it's just a game? Herewith, a list of some of those venues.

—Shirliey Fung

| VENUE | WHO PLAYS THERE | SPORT |
|---|---|---|
| Fleet Center | Boston Celtics | Basketball |
| | Boston Bruins | Hockey |
| Target Center | Minnesota Timberwolves | Basketball |
| United Center (United Airlines) | Chicago Bulls<br>Chicago Blackhawks | Basketball<br>Hockey |
| Continental Airlines Arena | New Jersey Nets | Basketball |
| | New Jersey Devils | Hockey |
| First Union Center | Philadelphia 76ers | Basketball |
| General Motors Place | Vancouver Grizzlies | Basketball |
| | Vancouver Canucks | Hockey |
| MCI Center | Washington Capitals | Hockey |
| | Washington Wizards | Basketball |
| Tropicana Field | Tampa Bay Devil Rays | Baseball |
| Ericsson Stadium | Carolina Panthers | Football |
| 3Com Park | San Francisco 49ers | Football |
| | San Francisco Giants * | Baseball |
| Coors Field | Colorado Rockies | Baseball |

* Editor's note: The Giants began playing at Pacific Bell Park on Opening Day 2000.

# Is It a Stadium or a Commercial?[5]

BY FILIP BONDY
*COLUMBIA JOURNALISM REVIEW*, JANUARY/FEBRUARY 2000

The Staples Center recently sparked a seething controversy at the *Los Angeles Times,* but sportswriters and editors have been wrestling with a subtler editorial dilemma over stadiums for decades: How do we identify sports arenas that have been christened or renamed by a sponsoring corporation?

Is it the Continental Airlines Arena in New Jersey, or the Meadowlands arena? Is it Qualcomm Stadium in San Diego, or Jack Murphy Stadium? Is it the Compaq Center in Houston, or the Summit? I know we are slowly losing this war, giving these sponsors their pound of publicity. I am just not sure about the journalistic rules of engagement.

Sports journalists tend to prefer to call sports facilities by their more familiar, historic names—if such a name exists. Readers relate to these old titles, we like to think. The old names often represent a geographic or conceptual link to the area. When Candlestick Park, home of the baseball Giants, suddenly declared itself "3Com Park," the *San Francisco Examiner* took a stand.

Sports editor Glenn Schwarz remembers going to his executive editor and explaining that the stadium had been known as Candlestick, or "The Stick," for more than thirty years, that it still was situated on Candlestick Point, and that it would always be known by readers as Candlestick. Despite some flak from a 3Com flack, the *Examiner* ran an editorial explaining that, as far as the paper was concerned, Candlestick would remain Candlestick. "We held out," Schwarz says.

This was all very noble. Unfortunately, the Giants will open a new stadium in April, PacBell Park, and there is no other name to use. *Examiner* sports columnist Ray Ratto is calling it "The Big Phone," but that may be a stretch.

At the *New York Daily News,* where I write, we called the home of the Nets and Devils "Meadowlands Arena" when it was officially "Brendan Byrne Arena," named after one of New Jersey's more obscure Democratic governors. We stuck to our guns when the place became "Continental Airlines Arena." Most of the other local papers applied the same, stubborn policy, although the *Newark*

5. Article by Filip Bondy from *Columbia Journalism Review* January/February 2000. Copyright © *Columbia Journalism Review.* Reprinted with permission.

*Star-Ledger* called the place by its fresh corporate name. My bosses snicker at this name, viewing it as a commercial intrusion in our copy. I tend to agree. But an argument for corporate freedom of expression could be made, too.

Here in the New York area, the Nets are planning to build a new arena in Newark, and the Devils hope to move to Hoboken. These new places are certain to get some unpronounceable, corporate tag.

All I ask for now is a little imagination in these sponsorships. I don't want the Knicks to sell their home court unless it is dubbed, "Dolly Madison Square Garden."

# Going to Extremes[6]

BY LAURA PETRECCA
*ADVERTISING AGE,* OCTOBER 11, 1999

Brett Cournoyer and two of his buddies drove several hours in a torrential downpour from Manchester, Conn., to Providence, R.I. Exhausted, they finally settled in at a local Marriott—not in a room, but in their compact car in the hotel's parking lot.

A short supply of cash and cramped sleeping quarters didn't dampen their spirits. The next morning, the trio were up early and ready to have some fun. As they wandered around a makeshift "interactive village" in this New England college town, it was clear the teen boys had no regrets about giving up their chance to sleep late on a Saturday morning.

"It's cool," said the 17-year-old Mr. Cournoyer as he wandered off to check out the newest BMX bikes.

Those two words are like alternative music to the ears of the executives who staged the Gravity Games in early September. The eight-day festival was NBC Sports' and Emap Petersen's answer to ESPN's lucrative X Games, and the latest attempt by media companies and marketers to reach into the hearts and surprisingly hefty wallets of the free-spending young male market.

### Freestyle Festival

Some 200,000 spectators descended on the Ocean State's capital city to watch more than 200 athletes participate in street luge, downhill skateboarding, wakeboarding and freestyle motocross competitions. And such brands as Mountain Dew, Doritos, Toyota, Hasbro Interactive, the U.S. Marines, Ultimate Speed Stick and Unionbay ponied up to $3 million apiece for top-tier, multimedia sponsorship packages.

"These are emerging sports, and we want to get in on the ground floor," said Bill Van de Graaf, a senior product manager at Colgate-Palmolive Co., marketer of Speed Stick.

NBC kicked off a month of taped coverage on Oct. 3. The first show scored a respectable 2.2 rating and 4 share opposite pro football. But while NBC's motivation was to make up for the loss of NFL broadcast rights, the Gravity Games aren't aimed at typical armchair quarterbacks.

---

6. Reprinted with permission from the October 11, 1999, issue of *Advertising Age*. 

That was obvious as Eric Buckland surveyed the bike course at the festival. He had been tipped off to check out the course by a friend who skipped school earlier in the week to attend the games.

"It's the best dirt jump course I've ever seen," said the 15-year-old from Franklin, Mass., who was clad in a Mountain Dew T-shirt and carrying a bag overflowing with free goodies from festival sponsors.

Eric was far from alone. Over the course of a week, tens of thousands of teen boys scarfed down jumbo hot dogs and gulped gallons of Mountain Dew as they rocked to the blaring sounds of the Amazing Crowns, Papa Vegas and Southern Culture on the Skids. All around them, young daredevils on skates, bikes and wakeboards performed tailwhips and grinds.

### Adrenaline Athletes

The music is called alternative and the sports extreme, but this is a cultural force clearly ready to burst into the mainstream.

***The music is called alternative and the sports extreme, but this is a cultural force clearly ready to burst into the mainstream.***

Among 12-to-24-year-olds, athletes such as Tony Hawk and Biker Sherlock are fast approaching the recognition level of Mark McGwire and Tiger Woods.

These stars aren't exactly the clean-cut, All-American types. When the games were canceled one day because of heavy rains, festival organizers secretly voiced concerns the young athletes would spend too much time partying and wouldn't be in shape to compete the next day.

But the adrenaline athletes are more accessible role models for the baggy-pants crowd, and they're beginning to show up as endorsers of everything from sneakers, sports drinks and fast-food to telecommunications products and automobiles.

Teen boys pack spending power estimated at $650 billion a year, and there are hundreds of marketers that each want their share. Sponsorship revenue for extreme sports reached $135 million last year, up from $24 million in 1993, according to IEG Sponsorship Report. Add in player endorsements, such as Mr. Sherlock's deal with sneaker marketer Converse, and the number soars even higher.

NBC's hope was to replicate the success ESPN has had with its X Games franchise. This year, 15 top-tier sponsors reportedly paid ESPN a total of $22 million for endorsement packages.

"We had been monitoring what ESPN was doing and were envious," said Kevin Monaghan, VP-business development at NBC Sports Ventures.

### Top-secret Mission

After it lost football, NBC went on the prowl for replacement programming. The network also was in search of ways to lure more young viewers.

In mid-1998, NBC assigned a dozen interns to a top-secret project. Their mission: to compile information on the market for extreme sports, even if it meant spying on ESPN. Most of the interns made calls under the guise of doing research for a school project.

They kept coming back with the name of a hot extreme athlete nicknamed Biker Sherlock. When a network executive realized the athlete was the son of NBC VP-Operations Mike Sherlock, everything clicked. The young Mr. Sherlock was soon signed on as a project consultant.

Unbeknownst to NBC, Emap Petersen's premerger Petersen unit was putting together plans for an extreme event of its own.

In August 1998, Petersen Chairman-CEO James Dunning presented the concept of an emerging-sports festival during a series of staff meetings. He had just purchased Gravity to fold into the company's Raw Sports Group and had an idea for a fabulous brand extension.

"Coming next year," Mr. Dunning headlined, "the Gravity Games on Fox or NBC."

Through sheer coincidence or serendipity, both NBC and Petersen turned to sports marketing specialist Advantage International to flesh out their concepts. Advantage, an Interpublic Group of Cos. unit since renamed Octagon Athlete Management, immediately saw a fit.

"In the beginning of October 1998, NBC and Petersen separately approached us about an emerging sports property," said Scott Seymour, Octagon VP-managing director of events. "With the two media powers, we thought it was best to combine them."

Top-level meetings were set up and, before the month was out, NBC and Petersen had joined forces.

### Marketer's Dream

"The deal was struck, cut and had the major points done in 72 hours," said Mr. Dunning, a diminutive dealmaker who resigned from Emap Petersen last week to return to the acquisition trail.

The fit between NBC and Petersen was a marketer's dream. NBC provided the production capabilities and, of course, the distribution platform in its broadcast network. Petersen, whose stable of magazines includes Dirt Rider, Skateboarder and Surfer, added credibility within the extreme sports market.

Both companies brought the marketing muscle to promote the event aggressively. Petersen placed ads in every issue of its young men's magazines, while NBC ran tune-in promos during pro basketball and college football broadcasts and in late-night and teen-oriented programming.

The partners set up a revenue sharing agreement under which Petersen assumed more risk—it spent about $20 million just to build the festival grounds—and therefore stood to gain more from the success of the event. They then set out to scout sites and sign up athletes.

Providence made an aggressive bid. It had hosted ESPN extreme events in the past and knew the economic impact of the event would be strong.

**Chaotic Scene**

At the festival's peak, the city was prowled by packs of tattooed teens carrying posters and bags filled with product samples. Outside the festival grounds, boys in hip-hugging jeans performed skateboard tricks on curbs and railings. The scene was chaotic, but it was exactly what Providence officials wanted, and why they worked so hard to beat out rival bids from Atlanta, Phoenix and San Diego.

"We tried to put together formidable proposal," said Gerard Martineau, majority leader of the Rhode Island House of Representatives. "This was a good business decision for us."

Providence will host the summer Gravity Games for the next three years, and city officials estimate they'll rake in upwards of $100 million.

**Divine Providence**

Mr. Dunning said Providence officials impressed the organizers with their flexibility.

"They said, 'We'll give you everything from the capital building to the civic center,'" Mr. Dunning said.

Providence isn't the only one that stands to gain. Mr. Dunning estimates the Gravity Games will add about $10 million a year in profits to Emap Petersen's coffers. He envisions a Gravity Games empire, complete with videogames, theme parks and branded music CDs.

Hasbro Interactive has already signed on to develop a Gravity videogame, and Pepsi-Cola Co., marketer of Mountain Dew, slapped the games' logo on the sides of 400 million 20-ounce soda bottles.

"I wouldn't be surprised if there was a Gravity soda," Mr. Dunning said.

For event sponsors, the Gravity Games represented a challenge as well as an opportunity. They were eager to capture young male eyeballs yet knew they had to move carefully to avoid alienating the marketing-savvy teens.

NBC and Petersen made room in the village for 70 tiny companies to hawk yo-yos and snowboards in hopes their street cred would rub off on the mega-marketers.

On the Saturday morning of the finals, Speed Stick's two big booths were neatly lined with 75,000 black-and-green deodorant samples. Colgate also hosted a photo shoot where festival visitors could have their photos superimposed on a mountain biking scene.

Across the way, Mountain Dew hosted athlete autograph sessions. Its white tent also served as the distribution center for the caffeine-laced soda, BBQ Doritos (a sibling product under PepsiCo) and free T-shirts.

**Extreme Marines**

Attendees also cued up at the U.S. Marines station to try out a chin-up bar. Some festival-goers raised a pierced eyebrow at the Marines' presence, but Lt. Colonel Ismael Ortiz assistant chief of staff-advertising, said sponsorship of extreme sports helps drive recruitment.

"These events reach our target audience, the 18-to-24-year-old," he said, adding, "We don't let the color of their hair or how they wear their clothes take away from who they are."

That aggressive youth marketing could be one reason the Marines are the only one of the major U.S. service branches that hasn't seen a steep decline in recruits.

"You've got to keep up with the times," Lt. Colonel Ortiz said. "We work hard to go out, build awareness and showcase what we do."

The ultimate success of the Gravity Games is by no means assured. Some skeptics believe extreme sports have a limited future. And NBC and Emap Petersen have to work hard to maintain credibility with young consumers who question the media giants' motives.

"NBC did it for the wrong reason. They did it for the money," said 18-year-old Steve Anderson, an extreme athlete from Keene State College, Keene, N.H., who attended the Gravity Games. "They just did it to cash out."

But cynicism aside, many of the teens who packed the event didn't seem to care who was behind the Gravity Games as long as there was plenty of action, food and music. And as long as they didn't have to dig too deeply into their wallets.

"The more free stuff, the better," said Eric Buckland, the Massachusetts teen, as he waved a tote filled with goodies. "We've got the bags to prove it."

Like, cool.

# VI. The Olympics

Elise Amendola/AP

*Venus Williams serves to opponent Henrieta Nagyova of Slovakia during the 2000 Olympics in Sydney, Australia. Williams went on to win the women's individual gold medal in tennis.*

# *Editor's Introduction*

The Olympic Games have always had a special mystique. Perhaps it is their infrequency, their taking place only once every four years, which gives them a sense of urgency for those athletes fortunate enough to compete in them. The saying "Wait till next year" does not apply to these Olympians, who might participate only once in their lifetimes. Few athletes have the longevity of a Carl Lewis, who competed in a remarkable four Olympic Games before his retirement. Most are more like Mark Spitz or Nadia Comaneci, electrifying the world with their record-setting performances in one memorable Olympics but prevented by age or injury (or both) from ever participating in another. The bravery of these Olympians can be astonishing, as when the marathoner on the verge of collapse makes that last lap around the stadium, or the gymnast with a sprained ankle finds a way to land her final vault to secure her team the gold medal. Though drug scandals and reports of corruption have somewhat dimmed the brightness of the Olympic flame, the Games continue to evolve and remain vital to world culture, as the articles in Section VI illustrate.

The first three pieces in the section celebrate the ideals of the Olympics and the gifted athletes who compete in them. Chris Privett's article "The Special Olympics: A Tradition of Excellence," describes how that organization prioritizes participation, effort, and friendship among its athletes, employing slogans such as "It's All About Attitude" to inspire them and positioning huggers at the finish line of every competition. Gold medalist Carl Lewis similarly emphasizes individual participants in his article "The Athletes Are the Games." While he acknowledges the serious problems with which the International Olympic Committee (IOC) still grapples, he reminds readers of the importance of supporting America's Olympians, who remain the "real stars of the Games." Cathy Harasta's article, "Women of the World," introduces readers to many of those stars, focusing specifically on the female athletes who are changing the face of Olympic sports and competition. Harasta explains how the 1996 Atlanta Games were a turning point for female Olympians by reviewing the performances of several U.S. teams, including gymnastics, basketball, softball, and soccer, before considering the women's chances at the 2000 Games in Sydney, Australia.

The final two articles in the section examine the major crises facing the Olympics today. In "World Strives to Purify Olympic Flame," Ilene R. Prusher and Ruth Walker and their colleagues examine the corruption and commercialism that plague the Olympic movement, from the manner in which the

IOC accepts bids from cities wishing to host the Games, to the sponsorship contracts made between large corporations and host nations, to the question of whether or not to hold the Games in nations with a history of human rights violations (such as China). The next article, "Drug Scandal Shines Spotlight on Image," by Bruce Horovitz, covers the other source of consternation for the IOC and Olympic athletes. The article reports on the 2000 Sydney Olympics, which saw a record number of Olympians disqualified either before or at the Games for using illegal performance-enhancing substances. Horovitz speculates on how this situation might affect the Games' future—including potential corporate sponsorship—and what measures the IOC could take to punish and prevent such intentional or inadvertent drug use by the athletes.

# The Special Olympics: A Tradition of Excellence[1]

BY CHRIS PRIVETT
*EXCEPTIONAL PARENT*, MAY 1999

Special Olympics athlete Sam Komanisi, from Special Olympics South Africa, began his address at an Athlete Congress dinner last year in Tanzania with these words: "The world may say I don't have a lot to give, but I have a gift to give you all here tonight. My gift is the gift of love. And I have another gift—it is the gift of friendship." Apart from demonstrating his skills as a toastmaster, Komanisi also proves one of Special Olympics firmest beliefs—that the athletes are the movement's most effective speakers. Every day, the athletes of Special Olympics shatter myths about the abilities of people who have mental retardation. This year, they will have plenty of opportunities to continue to showcase their abilities in the largest sporting event on earth.

On June 26, under the warm skies of Raleigh, North Carolina, Opening Ceremonies begin the nine days of competition of the 1999 Special Olympics World Games. The athletes in attendance will recite the Special Olympics oath: "Let me win. But if I cannot win, let me be brave in the attempt." That oath sums up the spirit of Special Olympics, a movement that has celebrated the heroic achievements of people who have mental retardation for more than 30 years.

## History of Achievement

Since 1968, Special Olympics athletes have been changing the world's attitudes about people who have mental retardation. Appropriately, the theme of the 1999 World Summer Games, "It's All About Attitude," reflects one of the goals of the Special Olympics movement: to shatter the stereotype that people who have mental retardation cannot compete. Over nine days between June 26 and July 4, 1999, in Raleigh-Durham-Chapel Hill, North Carolina, the world will see that Special Olympics athletes not only compete, they excel.

1. Article by Chris Privett from the *Exceptional Parent* May 1999. 

Special Olympics is more than just a once-every-four-years summer sports competition. It is a worldwide, year-round movement of sports training and competition that now includes more than one million athletes. World Games are held every two years, alternating between summer and winter games. For the 7,000 athletes who take part in the 1999 Special Olympics World Summer Games, the Games are the culmination of many months of training and local competitions.

Before the Games even begin, one million athletes will have given their best on playing fields in more than 150 countries in more than

***The philosophy behind Special Olympics is the belief that everyone deserves a chance to do his or her best, and that everyone can win.***

15,000 Special Olympics events in the last year. Those selected to attend the Games will have a place to compete and every opportunity to announce to the world, "I can do it!"

**Everyone Gets a Chance**

The philosophy behind Special Olympics is the belief that everyone deserves a chance to do his or her best, and that everyone can win. At Special Olympics, everyone makes the team—those who want to compete, can and do.

People are eligible to participate in Special Olympics if an agency or professional identifies them as having mental retardation, a cognitive delay, or significant learning or vocational problems, because of cognitive delay, requiring specially designed instruction. Athletes are eligible for training at age 5 and may begin competing on the day of their eighth birthday. "Divisioning," which groups athletes by age, sex, and ability, allows everyone to compete fairly.

Special Olympics offers a wide range of sports and events to accommodate athletes who have varying levels of mental abilities. Special Olympics follows International Governing Body rules for each of its sports, but also uses modifications to ensure that athletes have the best competitive experience.

Divisioning is the cornerstone of the program and it is used in all 25 official winter and summer sports offered by Special Olympics. This method is required at every level of Special Olympics competitions—local, national, regional, and global.

To provide the safest and most meaningful competitive experience possible, athletes compete against others who are close to them in age. The Official Special Olympics Rules recommend that there be no more than five years age difference between competitors. An athlete's age group is determined by his or her age on the opening day of the Games or competition. In team sports, the age of the oldest athlete on the team is used to determine the age group in which the team will compete.

Competitive divisions are structured so that athletes compete against others of similar ability. A fair and equitable division is one in which all participants, based on performance records, have a reasonable chance to excel. This divisioning can be determined using the 10 percent guideline, in which every effort is made to

***All Special Olympics athletes are given an equal opportunity to advance to the next level of competition—national, regional, or world games.***

place athletes in divisions where their performance ability is no more than 10 percent higher or lower than others.

All Special Olympics athletes are given an equal opportunity to advance to the next level of competition—national, regional, or world games. After local competition, the names of first place winners of all divisions are placed in a drawing. Names are then randomly selected and those athletes advance. It does not matter whether those first place winners have the fastest overall time.

### Success Beyond the Playing Field

The Special Olympics World Games offer the opportunity to showcase the abilities of people who have mental retardation. This new era of growth and innovation is being led by the athletes themselves, who are taking on leadership roles throughout the Special Olympics movement. Athletes now sit on boards of directors at the local, state, national, and international levels. They are also exploring other "non-traditional" roles through Athlete Leadership Programs (ALPs).

Thanks to ALPs, Special Olympics athletes around the world have stepped forward to let their voices be heard and their skills and talents shine. As trained and certified sports officials, some athletes have acted as umpires, referees, and coaches during competitions. As Global Messengers, they speak publicly at Special Olympics events, to civic, school, and business groups, and give interviews to the media.

One ALPs Program, the Special Olympics Officials Program for Athletes (SOOPA), trains and certifies athletes to serve as officials and skilled personnel at Special Olympics and other community sports competitions. One such athlete, Shannon Lamb of Indiana, hopes to be an official in figure skating at the Special Olympic's 2001 World Winter Games in Alaska, following her first experience as an athlete official at the 1997 Special Olympics World Winter Games in Toronto, Canada. "When I got home from the Games, I served as an official judge at the Indiana State Special Olympics Games," said Lamb. "I had a mentor to help me, but I did almost all of it myself."

Miguel Diaz, an athlete from Philadelphia, started out competing in Special Olympics, then decided to become a certified coach and softball official. "I like to share my skills and experience with other athletes who are starting out," said Diaz. Having grown up in a neighborhood rife with street gangs, Diaz is particularly proud of having achieved so much.

### Volunteers Make the Difference

Special Olympics athletes are indeed guiding the movement with bold new goals and innovative ideas. But the Special Olympics is, first and foremost, a sports movement. And it is the power of sports that enables Special Olympics to draw families together.

Several decades ago, it was not uncommon for people who have mental retardation to be excluded from society, and often kept in institutions. Today, however, the world is welcoming people who have mental retardation as vital, contributing members of communities and families. Families with a child who has mental retardation often feel thrust into situations that may make their daily lives more challenging. The Special Olympics offers families the opportunity to celebrate their athletes' achievements and to proudly share in the joys of sports training and competition, social interaction, and good old-fashioned family fun.

Families are Special Olympics' most powerful resource. They volunteer to help coach, transport, raise funds, officiate, chaperone, and train other volunteers. Families are the movement's most highly motivated and enthusiastic goodwill ambassadors. Simply put, Special Olympics would not exist today and could not have been created without the strong support of families around the world. The 1999 World Summer Games, for example, will enlist more than 35,000 volunteers in hosting the Games.

There are dozens of ways to volunteer for Special Olympics, from serving as coaches and trainers to offering to drive athletes to competitions or contributing typing, filing, or computer skills in Special Olympic offices. Even athletes who want to help Special Olympics athletes compete can get involved; the Special Olympics Unified Sports(TM) Program pairs athletes of similar abilities who have and do not have mental retardation, on the same sports teams.

Special Olympics volunteers learn very quickly that they are not only serving the movement, they are being served by it. It is not at all unusual to encounter a Special Olympics volunteer who will describe how much personal fulfillment one receives from interacting with Special Olympics athletes; for many volunteers, it is a commitment that endures throughout a lifetime.

North Carolina residents are also getting involved, taking advantage of a very hands-on volunteer opportunity by participating in the Special Olympics World Games Host Town Program. The Host Town Program provides housing for many Special Olympics athletes from outside the United States by inviting towns in the host state to "adopt" a particular nation's athletes during the Games. The Host Towns not only house and feed the athletes they "adopt," they also follow their adoptive athletes through the competitions, offering their cheers of support. More than 125 towns in North Carolina will be taking part in the Host Town Program during the 1999 World Games, marking the first formalized hosting program in the history of the World Games.

### Welcoming the World

The 1999 World Games represent the culmination of a year-long celebration of the 30th anniversary of the first Special Olympics games held in Chicago, Illinois, on July 20, 1968. At those first games, 1,000 athletes from the United States and Canada participated in aquatics, athletics (track and field), and floor hockey. In commemoration, and to mark the building of a bridge to a new generation of athletic heroes, Special Olympics Programs around the world have held a series of anniversary events over the past year, from China to the United Kingdom to South America. It is always exciting for Special Olympic athletes to represent their home countries during the World Games, but in 1999, several international Special Olympics Programs will be experiencing the thrill of the World Games for the very first time. Special Olympics is a worldwide movement that is always growing, always welcoming new members into the Special Olympics family. Among the Special Olympic Programs enjoying their inaugural World Games are Congo-Brazeville, Namibia, American Samoa, Yemen, and Lesotho.

### Being There

More than 1,000 US athletes will take part in the Cessna Special Olympics Airlift, courtesy of the Cessna Aircraft Company. Called the largest peacetime airlift in history, the Cessna Special Olympics Airlift will bring Special Olympics athletes from Team USA to North Carolina aboard hundreds of Cessna aircraft.

The Special Olympics World Games will offer everything sports fans would expect at a world-class sporting event: athletic skill, drama, compelling personal triumphs, record-breaking performances, and above all, fun. The World Games will include all of the breathtaking ceremony one would find at similar international sports competitions. Big-name entertainers will highlight the opening ceremonies and other celebrities will converge on Raleigh-Durham-Chapel Hill to admire some of their own personal heroes among the special athletes.

Spectators will find a myriad of memorable and exciting events at the 1999 World Games. Sports fans can get their fill of heart-pounding action at the competitions: aquatics, athletics, basketball, bocce, bowling, cycling, equestrian, football (soccer), golf, gymnastics, powerlifting, roller skating, softball, table tennis, team handball, tennis, and volleyball. There is also the World Games Festival, which will feature entertainment from top music acts, informational pavilions, and plenty of opportunities to meet some of the athletes.

Others may want to check out one of the two Olympic Towns being constructed. The Olympic Town at the Student Union of the UNC Chapel Hill campus will undoubtedly be the coolest place to be, in every sense of the word. Fully air-conditioned, it contains a bowling alley, a movie theater, and a "phone home" center.

Of course, the World Games are really just the beginning for the Special Olympics movement. The Special Olympics World Games will introduce millions of magazine and newspaper readers, television viewers, and sports fans to the heroic sports achievements of people who have mental retardation.

Beyond the World Games, the Special Olympics movement is changing lives every day around the world; Special Olympics athletes are changing hearts, minds, and attitudes. After the final whistle blows and the last race is run, that will be the greatest victory. That is what it is all about.

# "The Athletes Are the Games"[2]

BY CARL LEWIS
*NEWSWEEK*, FEBRUARY 15, 1999

Having retired from competition in 1997, I am no longer running and jumping my way around the world. I am now in the early stages of what I hope will be a successful acting career. But after representing the United States on five Olympic track-and-field teams—from 1980 to 1996—I certainly have a good feel for what the next class of Olympians is doing and thinking right now. For world-class athletes, the Olympic cycle is as eternal as the Olympic flame: First comes years of intense physical and mental preparation. Then there are private doubts and public challenges. And finally, if you are lucky enough to make it, there is the singular drama of Olympic competition. The ultimate joy comes from performing one's absolute best, no matter the order of finish.

This is what the Olympics should be all about. But now the headlines are being dominated by lurid tales of who paid how much to which members of the International Olympic Committee (IOC) and its inability to come to grips with the longstanding problem of drug use. Fortunately, the IOC's headaches have very little impact on the preparations of the world's greatest athletes for Sydney 2000 or Salt Lake City 2002. But they are a threat to the overall integrity of the Olympics, which is, after all, what makes the entire experience so special. We have to clean up the Olympics—everything from administration to competition—and keep them clean so that the Games can retain their mystique and incomparable glory.

Ultimately, the bribery allegations and investigations will be viewed as a temporary distraction. After all, the Olympics are not about the IOC's so-called "Lords of the Rings" or any other administrators. No, they are first and foremost about the athletes—from Jesse Owens to Muhammad Ali, from Mary Lou Retton to Jackie Joyner-Kersee—and about athletic achievement of the highest order. For me, the Olympics are embodied in one of my favorite passages from the Indian spiritual teacher Sri Chinmoy: "All athletes should bear in mind that they are competing not with other athletes but with their own capacities. Whatever I have already achieved, I have to go beyond." I turned to this notion whenever I needed an injection of competitive fire. Believe me, the joy that

2. Article by Carl Lewis from *Newsweek* February 15, 1999. 

comes from "going beyond" is the most incredible feeling in the world. I have felt it many times. And I have enjoyed watching others experience it.

Now, don't get me wrong. I'm certainly not naive enough to think that the Olympics are exclusively defined by that old rah-rah credo of faster, higher, stronger. Throughout my career, there was always at least one major uproar each Olympic year: political boycotts; drug scandals; the end of amateurism; the ever-expanding influence of TV and corporate sponsors, and, in 1996, the flap over Juan Antonio Samaranch's boast that the Olympic movement is "more important than the Catholic religion." Still, the controversies come and go. It's the athletes who form the grand continuum of the Games. Once they take center stage, all seems right again.

With that in mind we need to do several things for the athletes. We need to keep supporting their efforts—both financially and emotionally—despite any blemishes on the Olympic scene. We need to ensure that athletes have much greater input into major Olympic decisions, such as the choice of host cities, that have always been controlled by bureaucrats. We need to put current athletes, the people most affected by all these decisions, on all key committees. What's good for the athletes is good for competition and ultimately good for the fans.

Reliable drug testing is one of the most urgent issues facing the Olympics, because it only takes one cheating athlete to tarnish an entire competition. It can be an extraordinary distraction to settle into the starting blocks or prepare to launch oneself into the pool wondering if the person in the next lane might beat you because of something he or she ingested or injected.

If athletes had the deciding say in drug testing, we would no longer be debating the merits of an independent drug-testing lab, as the IOC is now doing. We would already have a more open, reliable and accountable system, including an independent lab that eliminates anyone with a vested interest from the process. (The IOC might have an incentive to cover up certain revelations so as not to detract from the Games.)

Another issue is what I call population control. With the IOC constantly adding sports—beach volleyball, mountain biking, ballroom dancing—the Games are feeling the crunch of overcrowding. Athletes are jammed into inadequate housing. Competition venues are forced further outside the host city. Security becomes a nightmare.

The IOC is supposedly considering many different reforms to clean up its traditionally unregulated house of gold. So this is the perfect time to consider a shift in the overall balance of power. If the IOC is indeed serious about turning its ongoing brouhaha into something positive, then let's make sure that the real stars of the Games—the athletes—emerge with something they can rally around.

# Women of the World[3]

BY CATHY HARASTA
*DALLAS MORNING NEWS,* AUGUST 27, 2000

Riding a 104-game winning streak, the USA women's softball team would appear bound for continued glory when the Sydney Olympic Games open next month.

Few teams in any sport, at any time, have dominated with the resounding authority of this fabulous 15. The USA women have not lost two games in a row in a major international competition since 1982. They rocketed through their pre-Olympic tour this summer, dubbed the "Central Park to Sydney" campaign. From the Big Apple through stops in Fort Worth and along the West Coast, the squad left crowds expecting another Olympics starring USA women's teams.

But the catch is that other nations are catching on in sports such as softball, which made its Olympic debut in 1996. Since the USA women won that gold medal, globalization has begun to define the next level in many of the team sports treasured by Americans.

Just as the Atlanta Games jump-started USA women's team sports, the Sydney Olympics, which begin Sept. 15, are expected to demonstrate other nations' strides in the past four years. The shrinking-planet concept has American women's teams bracing for challenges.

Christa Williams, the USA pitcher from the University of Texas, said defending the Olympic title will be no cinch.

"All the teams will be good—Australia, Canada, China, Cuba and Italy," she said. "There isn't a weak team this year."

American sports fans might not want to hear the immortal words of poet William Wordsworth: "The world is too much with us." But hear ye, anyway: The world is giving chase.

USA coaches, athletes and officials offered a number of explanations. Some pointed to America's lack of the high-performance sports centers that produce superstars in nations such as Australia and Russia. They also mentioned sports' governing bodies recruiting coaches from rival nations. And others cited technological strides, such as the ever-expanding Internet, which makes keeping tabs on farflung rivals easier and gives teams and players more exposure in all parts of the world.

---

3. Article by Cathy Harasta from the *Dallas Morning News* August 27, 2000. 

Women's athletics have mirrored other forms of sport, commerce and industry transformed by globalization, said Women's Sports Foundation president Nancy Lieberman-Cline, a former Olympic basketball player who coaches in the WNBA.

"With globalization, everything is getting more competitive," said Ms. Lieberman-Cline, whose team, the Detroit Shock, has four players from outside the United States. "Before, you really didn't know what anyone else was doing. When I need to know, I get on the Internet. We're sharing more with each other."

The refrain in Sydney might not exactly be *Bye, Bye, Ms. American Pie*. The USA still goes in as the favorite in several team sports. But International Olympic Committee vice president Anita DeFrantz,

***Women's athletics have mirrored other forms of sport, commerce and industry transformed by globalization.***

one of 13 women in the 113-member IOC, said USA women's teams will find it difficult to defend their Olympic championships.

No one is predicting a repeat of Atlanta, where American women's teams enjoyed unprecedented success. Team gold medals in basketball, gymnastics, soccer, softball and synchronized swimming galvanized a new level of acceptance of women's teams in America.

"It was huge," Ms. Williams said. "Now we're touring, and the fans are hungry for softball. The love of the sport has grown."

Previous Summer Olympics had given the world plenty of individual female stars such as gymnasts Nadia Comaneci in 1976 and Mary Lou Retton in 1984 and track and field standouts Wilma Rudolph in the 1956 and '60 Games and Jackie Joyner-Kersee in the 1980s and '90s.

But the Atlanta Olympics showcased team excellence and ignited a series of American successes: The WNBA launched in 1997. The USA won the inaugural women's ice hockey gold medal at the Nagano Olympics in 1998. And the USA soccer team defeated China in the sold-out Rose Bowl in the Women's World Cup in 1999.

Donna De Varona, an Olympic champion swimmer and veteran network sportscaster, said the big moments capture attention, but really are summations of many years of incremental success.

"Atlanta was a great breakthrough for the team sports," she said. "But those seeds were planted more than 25 years ago with Title IX."

Title IX, the 1972 federal law banning discrimination based on gender by institutions that accept federal funds, opened the door for more women's sports in colleges and high schools.

The boom was echoed in the Olympics. The number of women participating in the Games doubled from 1984–96, according to statistics compiled by the Women's Sports Foundation.

Since the Atlanta Games, women have made more strides that will show up in Sydney. The Australian Olympic Committee calculated 38 percent of the 10,400 Sydney Games athletes will be women—up from 34 percent in 1996.

In Sydney, for the first time, women will compete in the same number of team sports as men.

"When you look at sports added to the Olympic program, the noticeable trend of late is more opportunities emerging in sports for women," said Darryl Seibel, a spokesman for the U.S. Olympic Committee. "That's consistent with the trend we're seeing worldwide. One of the exciting things is the depth we're seeing worldwide in sports like softball and soccer. We now have trememdous competition in basketball. As women's sports continue to grow in popularity, that depth is important."

Ms. Lieberman-Cline said other nations have grown more familiar with the sports that USA women play best.

"When Australia has 10, 12 or 13 of its players playing in the WNBA, do you think they're afraid of Lisa Leslie?" Ms. Lieberman-Cline said, referring to the standout Los Angeles Sparks center who led the 1996 Olympic champion team in Atlanta. "In Sydney, there will be tremendous pressure on the U.S. to continue to win."

Just as corporate headhunters have gone global to fill important positions in industry, national Olympic organizations scour rival nations for talent.

The chance to turn mediocrity into a medal contender has coaches switching sidelines. Make that hemispheres, in Peggy Liddick's case.

Ms. Liddick has switched teams since the 1996 Olympics in Atlanta, where she helped coach the USA women to their first team gold medal in gymnastics. Then Australia wooed her to head a coaching staff that included fresh recruits from Russia and China. Such coaching carousels suggest the global balance of power will be increasingly subject to change.

The Aussies, buoyed by their meteoric rise in gymnastics, sniff a medal in a sport that never had been a strength for them. They finished fifth at the World Championships in China last year, in a competition dominated by traditional powers Romania and Russia.

The USA finished sixth—a far cry from their triumph in Atlanta, where the team produced the all-time top U.S. showing for a non-boycotted Games.

The squad won five medals in Atlanta. Then all but one member retired from high-level competition.

The drop from 1996 Olympic champions to sixth place in the world so alarmed USA Gymnastics officials that they lured Bela Karolyi out of retirement last November. What first sounded like a radical response turned out to be a reasonable reaction to globalization's impact.

The former Olympic coach, a native of Romania who defected to the United States in 1981, assumed coordination of the women's program to shape up the team for Sydney.

Mr. Karolyi began holding monthly training camps for the Olympic hopefuls at his New Waverly, Texas, ranch. He stressed the discipline and confidence visible in Russian and Romanian teams when they arrive at meets. He deliberately ran some camp sessions as if they were competitions to prepare the athletes for stronger opponents and unforgiving international judges.

***"The noticeable trend of late is more opportunities emerging in sports for women."—*** **Darryl Seibel, the U.S. Olympic Committee.**

In April, an international meet in New Zealand that the Americans won gave them a taste of what Sydney will be like in terms of unsympathetic crowds.

"New Zealand is a beautiful island," said Mr. Karolyi, who coached 28 Olympic gymnasts, "but it was hostile for us."

Nell Fortner, coach of the USA women's Olympic basketball team, said her squad also will find Sydney far different from Atlanta's packed and partisan Georgia Dome. The gold-medal performance in 1996 served as a springboard for the WNBA, which launched the next year.

"There's no comparison to 1996," Ms. Fortner said. "Basketball is turning into a global sport. We're continuing to grow the game. There's a lot more room to grow. Now we have a professional league that will only get better."

The 1996 USA basketball team won 59 consecutive games before topping Brazil for the championship, its third title in the last four Olympics. Ms. Fortner said just as Atlanta awakened many people to the excitement of women's basketball, Sydney will expand the game's horizons.

"Maybe you'll see where people will have more respect for foreign players," said Ms. Fortner, whose new job as head coach-general manager of the WNBA's Indiana team begins after the Olympics. "I think you'll see players become better players faster. It's the responsibility of all of us to make our product better. That's the spirit of competition."

One athlete certain to help the reputation of international women basketball players is Australia's Lauren Jackson, who could join American track and field star Marion Jones among the signature faces of the Sydney Games. Ms. Jones is aiming to win five gold medals in Sydney. Ms. Jackson, 18, is a 6-5 center who probably will play in the WNBA next year.

Ms. Leslie, a center on the USA Olympic team, called Ms. Jackson the "best player outside the United States." In the Australian newspapers, she has been called the best player since Michael Jordan retired.

Ms. Fortner pointed out that Ms. Jackson has had the benefit of training at the Australian Institute of Sport. The AIS is a large, government-funded facility with athletes from many sports on scholarships.

The specialized setting of a sports institute exposes a young athlete to top coaching and to other highly motivated competitors in ways the United States colleges can't match, said Chris Carver, coach of the USA Olympic Synchronized Swimming Team.

"What has happened is that the rest of the world has developed high performance centers, meaning a lot of other countries have a lot more available than we do," Ms. Carver said. "The French have had the Sports Institute in Paris since the 1980s. Now we see Italy getting one, and Spain. We have to work within various schools here and put our resources into private clubs."

Ms. Carver said her team has learned much from member Anna Kozlova, a native of St. Petersburg, Russia, who became a United States citizen last fall. Her father directs the swimming program at the Academy of Physical Education in Russia.

"For Anna, education and sport went together," Ms. Carver said. "Russian athletes are very powerful. They're trained better as young people."

In April, the USA finished fourth at the Olympic Games Qualifying Event, won by Russia, in Sydney.

"Fourth was not what we had hoped for," said Ms. Carver, in her 39th year of coaching synchronized swimming. "We rewrote our program after that. In Sydney, it will be very, very tough to defend the [Olympic] title. But we sort of relish the challenge."

The Sydney Games will mark 100 years of women's Olympic participation. Ms. DeFrantz, one of three IOC members from the United States, said globalization is older than it might seem in women's sports. She said women's sports received more attention in the United States because of the Atlanta Games. Around the world, she said, women athletes long have trained and competed without much exposure to American sports fans.

"Women's sports were always there," said Ms. DeFrantz, an Olympic rowing medalist in 1976. "No one wrote about them."

NBC, which will televise the Olympics in the USA, has guaranteed that viewers will see plenty of womens sports.

In Sydney, women will compete for the first time in a number of new sports, including tae kwon do, triathlon, modern pentathlon, water polo, weightlifting, trampoline and pole vault.

Though progress on the field has been steady, Ms. DeFrantz said women's athletics must expand its scope.

"We have more work to do among administrators—getting women in those roles," she said.

Ms. De Varona, co-founder of the Women's Sports Foundation in 1974–75 and chairwoman of the Women's World Cup in soccer last year, said the feel-good moments must be recognized for the amount of off-the-field legwork they embody. She said she loved every second of sitting in the Rose Bowl and watching the USA beat China in the World Cup.

"It was just an exclamation point," she said. "With all women in sport, it's just one little step at a time that adds up."

Nicole Vollebregt, director of public relations for Beaverton, Oregon-based Adidas America, said she sees globalization's effects when children in other countries seek autographs from USA women soccer players. Adidas, a sportswear and athletic shoe manufacturer, is the official outfitter of the U.S. Olympic Team. She said Adidas has been involved in women's soccer for 30 years.

"The trend that started in the U.S. has been growing globally," Ms. Vollebregt said. "You had 92,000 people in the Rose Bowl for the Women's World Cup final. Soccer has grown in the United Kingdom, Germany, Sweden, Asia and Scandinavia. Companies are starting to see that women are marketable as athletes, and not just the figure skaters and gymnasts. And it's going to be increasingly OK for women to participate in the sports men compete in."

A women's professional soccer league will launch in eight American cities in April. Unlike the WNBA, which is under the NBA's auspices, the new soccer league will not have a "father" figure.

Said Ms. De Varona: "For women's soccer, it truly is a league of their own."

She said it will add a chapter to a long story, one that has global ramifications. "We've raised the bar in soccer around the world," she said.

In doing so, the USA soccer squad has taken its lumps, losing three times in the past year to Norway—the first nation the Americans will face in the Sydney Games.

That's the price of globalization.

You win some. You lose some.

# World Strives to Purify Olympic Flame[4]

BY ILENE R. PRUSHER, RUTH WALKER ET AL
*CHRISTIAN SCIENCE MONITOR*, FEBRUARY 24, 1999

If Zeus could see them now.

Given the lasting furor around the International Olympic Committee, the gods of Greek mythology might lumber down from Mt. Olympus to rekindle the spirit in which the Games were begun.

As it is, modern Greece is making an effort to do so. So are a host of other nations.

No corruption, less commercialism, and a cease-fire in the world's wars are some of the high goals Greek organizers are setting as Athens prepares to host the Olympics in August 2004—for the first time since the ancient games were revived here in 1896.

To varying degrees, calls for a back-to-basics approach are being issued worldwide. Events throughout the history of the Games have stolen the spotlight from sport: terrorism, boycotts, the use of performance-boosting drugs.

But none has generated as great a call for reinvigorating the Olympic tradition as the furor around Salt Lake City's vote-buying in securing the right to play host in 2002.

Toronto has appointed an ethics commissioner in its bid for 2008. Beijing, despite sharp words aimed at Sydney over the rights to 2000, has sided with Australians rather than trying to use controversy to wrest the Games away. And in Mexico City, one idea involves having rich nations help poor ones play host.

In Greece, some politicians have revived the idea of permanently bringing the Olympics back to their homeland as a way of putting a stop to the graft that has come to be associated with the act of moving the Games from one country to another.

But the proposal by Greece's right-wing New Democracy Party was rejected Feb. 10 in the European Parliament, and is even being dismissed as "romantic" by Costas Bakouris, the Greek business executive in charge of getting Athens into shape for the Olympics in 2004.

---

4. This article first appeared in the electronic edition of *The Christian Science Monitor* on February 14, 1999, and is reproduced with permission. 

"We're trying to do everything we can to make it more democratic and transparent," says Mr. Bakouris, who was recruited for the top job by Greece's prime minister. "We want to give it the historical balance that only Greece can give."

The Greek Ministry of Sports will hold a Youth Festival earlier that summer at the actual site of ancient Olympia with 4,000 athletes under the age of 18 forsaking beach volleyball and the like for classic Olympic events.

Greece will also try to institute a cultural Olympiad between 2000 and 2004. This new period of international cultural exchange would be hosted by whichever country was holding the Olympics.

And, most boldly, Athens 2004 and the Greek Foreign Ministry are trying to revive the idea of an Olympic-inspired military truce to recapture the nonbelligerence competitors agreed to during the ancient Games.

"We, of course, cannot stop war," says Jacques Rogge, a Belgian who serves as the International Olympic Committee's (IOC) coordinating chairman for the Sydney 2000 and Athens 2004 Games. "We can just relay the ideal of the Games to . . . world leaders, but ultimately we depend on the goodwill of politicians and governments."

What could prove just as difficult is scaling back commercial endorsements. Many sponsorship contracts have already been given out. And the idea of limiting profits may be a hard sell in Greece, the poorest member of the European Union.

Bakouris insists he will have limits: "We won't commercialize the torch relay," he says, criticizing Coca-Cola's place on the back of the torch-bearer's T-shirt at the 1996 Olympics in Atlanta.

"If they want to do that, they can hang me from the Acropolis," he says.

Elsewhere, the desire to win the Games somewhere down the line appears undimmed, though a new care is being applied to bringing them in.

### Toronto's "City-building" Hopes

Bid organizers in Toronto express hope that whatever reforms within the Olympic movement are introduced in the wake of the current corruption scandal will only work to Toronto's benefit as it seeks to win the 2008 Games.

Before the scandal over the selection of Salt Lake City for the 2002 Winter Games, TO-Bid Committee chairman David Crombie says, the conventional wisdom was that Toronto's approach to wooing the Games was too high-minded to be effective.

"They kept saying to me, 'You're going to look too much like a Boy Scout,'" he says. "Well, maybe they'll be looking for some Boy Scoutism now."

In the near term, Mr. Crombie, a former mayor of Toronto, says, "there will inevitably be some confusion as to what the rules of engagement are." The site of the 2006 Winter Games will be chosen this July, on the basis of new rules to be officially introduced in March, he notes.

Competition for the 2008 Games doesn't officially open until this fall, and so the IOC and the prospective host cities will have a chance to go through a complete cycle under the new rules before Toronto has its turn to compete, he adds.

Inevitably, he suggests, there will be modifications to the new rules that will govern selection of the 2006 site. And the problems within the Olympic movement, which he refers to as a "culture going through some crises," may take some time to clear up.

The TO-Bid Committee has just announced the appointment of its ethics commissioner: Charles Dubin, a former chief justice of Ontario who led an inquiry into the doping scandal involving runner Ben Johnson in 1989.

One of Crombie's other hats is as chair of the Waterfront Regeneration Trust, which aims to redevelop Toronto's Lake Ontario waterfront, the site the bid committee has in mind for the Games. Crombie sees a great opportunity for "city building" if Toronto does win the Games.

The 1976 Games in Montreal offered a similar city-building opportunity there, but Jean-Claude Marsant, an architect and University of Montreal professor, suggests that the opportunity was largely muffed. Nine years before the Games, Montreal had hosted Expo '67, the occasion for building the subway system and other infrastructure, as well as a new stadium—which was subsequently torn down. Professor Marsant laments that the Olympic construction program didn't build on Expo's but rather was located farther away from the city center.

The Olympic Village, a "mixed blessing," in Marsant's view, is still in use for mixed-income housing. "It's worked reasonably well, but it's so isolated, sort of out there in a field. Housing like that really should be more integrated in the city."

### Sydney Recalls Melbourne Success

Meanwhile, in Australia, Sydneysiders are having to come to terms with revelations that their own bid for the 2000 Games was not as aboveboard as they thought. But, however their Games play out, they are unlikely to provide the same kind of coming-of-age moment for Sydney as the 1956 Games afforded to Melbourne.

Melbourne at midcentury was painfully conscious of its remoteness and backwardness; its people worried what their international visitors would think of them.

In the end, it is widely agreed, it all worked out. David Studham, librarian of the Melbourne Cricket Club, one of the principal venues for the Games, says: "The real benefits, I believe, were cultural. . . . The Olympics had a great effect on the start of multicultural Melbourne." He cites culinary diversity as one benefit.

"One other major social legacy of the Olympic Games is television. It was finally introduced into Australia for the Games."

**Europe's Pocketbook Approach**

The recent corruption scandals may have dimmed the Games' popular appeal in much of Europe, but officials in major towns all across the Continent are as eager as ever to host the biggest show on earth.

Paris, Seville in Spain, and Istanbul have already thrown their hats in the ring for the 2008 Summer Games, and other cities such as London and Manchester in England are still considering putting their names forward.

***The problems within the Olympic movement . . . may take some time to clear up.***

"The Olympic Games give a formidable boost to the economy, the tourist industry, and the image of any city," says Jean-Pierre Labro, spokesman for Paris Mayor Jean Tiberi.

"The problems with doping and corruption don't stain the image of the Olympics themselves, just some of the organizers," he adds. "What's happening today has not reduced our interest in hosting the Games one bit."

"These are ancient Games," says Jane Price, a sports official with Manchester City Council. "You go through hiccups in the evolution of any organization, and hopefully this is just one of those hiccups."

At the moment, though, the things that have gone wrong with the Olympic Games are uppermost in many minds. "Who knows, maybe Paris has already been chosen for 2008," joked Magaline Vermalet, a provincial municipal employee visiting the French capital on Tuesday. "With all the corruption that swayed the last few choices, who knows?"

Some Paris residents are also worried about the cost: Three-quarters of the investment needed to host the Olympics here would be borne by central and local government. "If the Games are held in Paris we'll see it in our tax bills," warns pensioner Macelle Laville. "I've got a friend in Grenoble and she's still paying for the 1968 Winter Games."

But for city officials, the price is worth paying. "Just going through the process of applying [for the 2000 Olympics in a failed bid] improves the confidence and morale of a city," says Ms. Price. "We attracted a huge amount of publicity and we put Manchester on the world map."

**Different Lines from Beijing**

Chinese citizens and media are lashing out at the IOC scandal and the possibility that Beijing narrowly lost its bid to host the 2000 Olympics because of Australian vote-buying: Sydney beat out Beijing by two votes in the International Olympic Committee's 1993 vote on who would host the so-called millennial Games.

China's state-controlled television and newspapers have given wide coverage to charges that an Australian businessman funneled more than $30,000 each to two IOC delegates on the eve of the vote.

"The Chinese Olympic Committee should strongly protest the scandal, and ask for a new vote on whether Beijing should host the 2000 Olympics," says a Beijing taxi driver surnamed Li.

While Mr Li's proposal is being echoed across the Chinese capital, it is being muted in Beijing's corridors of power.

Chinese officials instead are focusing on Beijing's new application to stage the 2008 Olympiad, and voicing support for the IOC's decision not to strip Sydney or Salt Lake City of the right to host the Games because of bribery allegations.

The official newspaper *China Daily* recently quoted a China Olympic Committee leader as saying, "The two host cities have made huge efforts to prepare for the Games, and should not be denied due to several [IOC] members' misconduct."

But the newspaper added in an editorial that "The IOC bribe-takers have shown us that trading power and rules for favors is rampant," and it called for a "thorough house-cleaning" and "serious soul-searching" within the IOC's leadership.

Beijing is unlikely to press for a new vote on the 2000 Olympics now, when the authorities are orchestrating a crackdown on the fledgling opposition China Democracy Party.

On the eve of the IOC's vote on Beijing's first bid six years ago, the US House of Representatives passed a resolution urging the sports body to reject China's candidacy because of its widespread human rights abuses.

Yet most pro-democracy activists here say they strongly support Beijing's efforts to stage the 2008 Olympics.

"Allowing Beijing to stage the Olympics will accelerate China's integration into global society," says Bao Tong, the most senior Chinese official to be imprisoned for allegedly backing democracy-demonstrations here in 1989.

Mr. Bao, onetime secretary to the Communist Party's all-powerful Politburo, adds that "awarding Beijing the Games will strengthen those who back political reform within the party and open China to observers from all over the globe."

---

***"Allowing Beijing to stage the Olympics will accelerate China's integration into global society."*—Bao Tong, a pro-democracy senior Chinese official.**

---

**For Japan, It's the Economy**

The Olympics have been good to Japan. The 18th Olympiad was held in Tokyo in 1964—giving the country a chance to shine on the world stage less than two decades after the end of World War II. People here took pride in showing off a rebuilt and technologically advanced country.

Just eight years later, the city of Sapporo was the first Asian city to host the winter Games, underscoring Japan's return to the community of nations.

But Japan's more recent attempts at Olympic-hosting glory—the winter Games at Nagano last year and Osaka's bid to host the 2008 Summer Games—have had more to do with local economic ambition than celebrating national achievement.

The world may never know just what the Nagano bid committee did to win the right to host the Games, thanks to the incineration of key documents in 1992, but intimations of bribery and influence-peddling haven't shocked too many Japanese. This is a culture where lavish entertainment and gift-giving are routine; many Japanese are much more upset about government officials receiving such largesse.

Even so, a handful of critics here say the entire movement has become too corrupt and should be disbanded.

"I heard from many people that they were very disappointed at the beginning [of the IOC scandal], but they also realized that they . . . were only disappointed with the management of the IOC and not with the Olympics itself," says Tetsuo Oyama, an official of the Japan Olympic Committee.

Mr. Oyama says he understands the motivation behind proposals to host the Games in Athens, but disagrees. "As represented in those five circles, the site should move from one place to another over different continents. We learn a lot about other countries that way."

**Mexico City Calls for Openness**

At the Mexican Olympic Committee's headquarters and training

***"The damage done . . . reinforces the idea that the Olympics' values are being lost."***—
**bronze medalist Bernardo Segura.**

grounds in Mexico City, the athletes aren't too busy to enter a lively discussion on corruption in the IOC and the role of money in the Olympics in general.

The image of the world's greatest sports event is tarnished and damage has been done, all agree. But solutions do exist for returning to the Games their luster, athletes and trainers say—starting with a greater democracy and transparency in the Olympics' governance.

"The damage done affects all of us, because it reinforces the idea that the Olympics' values are being lost," says Bernardo Segura, a bronze medalist in distance walking at the Atlanta Games. "One danger is that sponsors will consider the Games' reputation so blackened that they will stay away, and that will hurt everybody."

The dismissal of six IOC members was the correct "initial" action to be taken, Mr. Segura says, but a more extensive "cleanup" is necessary, he adds, and one that is not carried out behind closed doors.

"Everybody knew the corruption existed, and the only way to demonstrate to the public that it's being weeded out is to be more open," he says.

Mexico City's summer Games of 1968—the only time the Games have been held in Latin America—are remembered by many Mexicans with great pride, as they offered Mexico the opportunity to strut its accomplishments as a modernizing oil power on the world stage.

That pride is clouded by the memory of violent disturbances that pitted university students against soldiers in the weeks before the Games. The protests weren't directly aimed at the Games, but many historians believe the government's fear of seeing its big international moment disrupted was at the origin of its deadly repression.

Despite those events the Games were positive for Mexico in a way that shouldn't be denied other countries, especially the world's less wealthy ones, many observers in Mexico say. "The '68 Games remain a source of pride for Mexicans just as much of the sports facilities built around the city [for the Games] remain in heavy use," says Jose Arturo Isunza, chief spokesman for the Mexican government's National Sports Commission.

Giving the Games a permanent home, as some critics of the site-selection process have suggested, would also diminish their cultural dimension and the opportunity for thousands of athletes, spectators, and TV viewers to get to know different parts of the world. For Pedro Aroche, a trainer with Mexico's walking team, the answer is to establish a rotation among the world's continents for hosting the Games.

"Why not establish a fund where the richest countries would help the poorer to pay for hosting the Games?" asks Mr. Aroche. "That way the same international solidarity that is behind the Games would also be part of their location."

# Drug Scandal Shines Spotlight on Image[5]

BY BRUCE HOROVITZ
*USA TODAY*, SEPTEMBER 28, 2000

An Olympic Games tainted by banned drug use is giving long-time Olympic sponsors the willies. And it is leaving marketers wondering if this—and not the bribery scandal involving potential host cities—is now the critical hurdle facing the Olympic image.

As the use of banned drugs has emerged as a front-and-center story of the Sydney Games, fear of the next drug-related bombshell has sponsors in a quiet tizzy. Some major sponsors—IBM, UPS and Kodak among them—say the International Olympic Committee must deal with the drug issue head-on.

"The Olympics always have been about the purity of sports," says Manny Rivera, director of corporate partnerships for Kodak, which has been an Olympic sponsor for 104 years. "Drug use will become an increasingly important issue that the IOC will have to address."

The question seems not to be if, but when, another high-profile athlete will be in the headlines.

This week, world track-and-field officials said shot-putter C. J. Hunter, husband of gold medal sprinter Marion Jones, tested positive before the Games for a steroid. The IOC then said the 1999 world champion had failed three other tests. Hunter did not compete here, withdrawing from the U.S. team two weeks ago because of knee surgery. He denied the charges.

To date, a record 35 Olympic athletes—from Bulgarian weightlifters to Egyptian wrestlers—have been removed from competition for using performance-enhancing drugs. By comparison, just two drug cheats were removed from the Atlanta Games.

No Olympic sponsors have defected yet. None are even rattling sabers. And no marketer has dropped Olympic athletes. But there's a clear concern among sports marketers that, for all practical purposes, the image of the Games—and Olympic athletes—has just taken a javelin in the heart.

"Until now, the Olympic scandals managed to miss the athletes," says David Carter, a sports marketing professor at the University of Southern California. "But this makes the athletes look no better than the rest of the cronies."

If drug use harms consumers' perception of the Olympics, "it will be harder for sponsors to justify the huge expense," says Sean Brenner, managing editor of the newsletter *IEG Sponsorship Report.*

Nike, the company most directly affected by Hunter's situation, is keeping a low profile on the drug issue. Hunter is paid to wear Nike gear. Jones is one of Nike's highest-profile endorsers.

"Nike follows a standard that presumes innocence until proven guilty when an athlete is claimed to have used a banned substance," the company said in a statement. "As such, we stand by C. J. Hunter during this very difficult time."

Nike is a Sydney sponsor, though it is not one of the 11 global Olympic sponsors. Nike also is a key sponsor of USA Track & Field.

"Nike does not advocate or condone doping," spokesman Lee Weinstein says. "Doping is a serious matter and could result in the termination of a team's or individual athlete's agreement with Nike."

Most major sponsors have ethics clauses etched into their contracts that would technically give them an out if drugs tarnish the Games in a big way.

But clearly they are not happy that drugs are even an issue.

UPS, the only worldwide sponsor that hasn't renewed, is watching with keen interest. "We're concerned about anything that would compromise the integrity of the Games," says spokeswoman Susan Rosenberg. "But it (the drug issue) is not something we're ready to take a defining position on."

Xerox, a sponsor of the Olympics and USA Track & Field, wants the IOC to bring all the facts forward. "Let's get everything out in the open," says Terry Dillman, Olympics marketing manager. "Then we can get beyond it."

## Olympic Doping Cases

*USA Today,* October 1, 2000

### DISQUALIFIED AT GAMES

**Ashot Danielyan, Armenia, weightlifter:** Lost bronze medal in the heavyweight division after testing positive for steroids. Two other non-medalists also were nabbed for drugs on the final day of competition.

**Fritz Aanes, Norway, Greco-Roman wrestler:** Tested positive for nandrolone after losing a bronze-medal match.

**Andreea Raducan, Romania, gymnast:** Lost all-around gold medal on Tuesday after test found pseudoephedrine, apparently from cold pills.

**Ioachim Oana, Romania, physician:** Banned through 2004 Games.

**Andris Reinholds, Latvia, rower:** Tested positive for banned steroid nandrolone, expelled from Olympics on Saturday. Finished ninth in men's single sculls. Blamed Chinese herbal medicine.

**Izabela Dragneva, Bulgaria, weightlifter:** Stripped of gold medal at 105 pounds on Friday after test found furosemide, a banned diuretic

**Sevdalin Minchev, Bulgaria, weightlifter:** Stripped of bronze medal in the men's 137-pound class on Friday, furosemide.

**Ivan Ivanov, Bulgaria, weightlifter:** Loses silver medal in 123 pound class on Sept. 20, furosemide. Won gold medal at 1992 Barcelona Olympics

**Svetlana Pospelova, Russia, 400-meter runner:** Tested positive for the steroid stanozolol in an out-of-competition test.

### DISQUALIFIED IN SYDNEY, PRE-COMPETITION TESTS

**Traian Ciharean and Adrian Mateas, Romania, weightlifting:** Expelled Sept. 15 for positive tests before competition. Ciharean won bronze medal at Barcelona.

**Vadim Devyatovsky, Belarus, hammer throw:** Expelled Sept. 20. Positive test for nandrolone on Sept. 12.

**Chen Po-pu, Taiwan, weightlifter:** Tested positive on Aug. 28.

**Dieter Baumann, German runner:** Gold medalist in 5,000 meters at Barcelona, suspended on Sept. 18 for 1999 tests for nandrolone. Claims toothpaste was spiked.

**Alexander Bagach, Ukraine, shot put:** 1996 Olympic bronze medalist, suspended Sept. 19 for Feb. 12 steroid test.

**Simon Kemboi, Kenya, runner:** Banned Sept. 19 for Sept. 12 nandrolone test.

### DISQUALIFIED BEFORE REACHING SYDNEY

**China** cut 27 athletes from Olympic team early in September, most for positive drug tests.

**Jan Hruska, Czech cyclist:** Nandrolone, Sept. 13 during Tour of Spain.

**Zbynek Vacura, Czech weightlifter:** Sent home while en route to Sydney. Aug. 9 test showed dehydroepiandrosteron, an anabolic steroid.

**Robin Lyons, Canada, hammer-throw:** Norandrosterone, a metabolite of nandrolone, at Canadian Olympic trials in August. Blamed diet supplement.

**Eric Lamaze, Canada, show jumper:** Second ban for positive cocaine test.

**Neil Campbell, Britain, cyclist:** Tests at World Cup meeting in Turin, Italy, on July 13 and at British Championships on July 29 showed elevated concentrations of human chorionic gonadotrophin (HCG).

**Iva Prandzheva, Bulgaria, triple and long jump:** Banned on Sept. 13 following nandrolone test.

**Yevgenyia Yermakova, Kazakstan, swimmer:** Furosemide found at meet in Monte Carlo in May.

**Chen Jui-lien and Wu Mei-yi, Taiwan, weightlifting:** Steroids found in March. Chen was a 1999 women's world champion.

**Tammy Thomas, cyclist:** High testosterone level found after April 29 Olympic trial.

**Linford Christie, Britain, sprinter:** 1992 gold medalist at 100 meters banned as coach for nandrolone test in early 1999.

**Doug Walker, Britain, runner:** Banned in August for nandrolone test.

**Dupe Osime, Nigeria, 800-meter runner:** initially chosen for Nigeria's Olympic team but not brought to Sydney, tested positive for steroids in an out-of-competition test.

## RELATED CASES

**C. J. Hunter, U.S. shot put:** IOC officials say he tested positive for nandrolone during summer. Lost Olympic credential. World champion and husband of U.S. runner **Marion Jones**, he was not entered for Olympics, citing knee injury. Blames diet supplement.

**Merlene Ottey, Jamaica, sprinter:** Banned after positive test for nandrolone in July 1999. Reinstated after finding sample improperly tested and blamed diet supplement. Competed in Sydney but failed to win medal.

**Mark Richardson, Britain, runner:** Withdrew in early September while fighting attempt to ban him for nandrolone test.

**Javier Sotomayor, Cuba, high jumper:** Tested positive for cocaine at 1998 Pan American Games. Four-year suspension cut to two years on appeal. Won silver medal in Sydney. Denied using cocaine.

**Sergei Voynov, Uzbekistan, coach:** Fined $5,500 for trying to bring human growth hormone into Australia before the Olympics. Claimed was treating own skin problem.

# Bibliography


Averbuch, Gloria, and Ashley Michael Hammond. *Goal!: The Ultimate Guide for Soccer Moms and Dads.* Emmaus, PA: Rodale P, 1999.

Berkow, Ira. *Court Vision: Unexpected Views on the Lure of Basketball.* New York: William Morrow & Company, 2000.

Bodo, Peter. *The Courts of Babylon: Tales of Greed and Glory in a Harsh New World of Professional Tennis.* New York: Scribner, 1995.

Bowen, William G., and James L. Shulman. *The Game of Life: College Sports and Educational Values.* Princeton: Princeton UP, 2001.

Cagan, Joanna, and Neil De Mause. *Field of Schemes: How the Great Stadium Swindle Turns Public Money into Private Profit.* Monroe, ME: Common Courage P, 1998.

Costas, Bob. *Fair Ball: A Fan's Case for Baseball.* New York: Broadway Books, 2000.

Currie, Stephen. *The Olympic Games.* San Diego: Lucent Books, 1999.

Fox, Stephen R. *Big Leagues: Professional Baseball, Football, and Basketball in National Memory.* Lincoln: U of Nebraska P, 1998.

Hauser, Thomas. *The Black Lights: Inside the World of Professional Boxing.* Fayetteville: U of Arkansas P, 2000.

Kahn, Roger. *A Flame of Pure Fire: Jack Dempsey and the Roaring 20s.* New York: Harcourt Brace, 1999.

———. *The Head Game: Baseball Seen from the Pitcher's Mound.* New York: Harcourt Brace, 2000.

Karinch, Maryann. *Lessons from the Edge: Extreme Athletes Show You How to Take on High Risk and Succeed.* New York: Simon & Schuster, 2000.

Lenskyj, Helen Jefferson. *Inside the Olympic Industry: Power, Politics, and Activism.* Albany: SUNY Press, 2000.

Longman, Jere. *The Girls of Summer: The U.S. Women's Soccer Team and How It Changed the World.* New York: HarperCollins, 2000.

Lupica, Mike. *Mad As Hell: How Sports Got Away from the Fans—And How We Get It Back.* Lincolnwood, IL: Contemporary Publishing, 1997.

———. *Summer of '98: When Homers Flew, Records Fell, and Baseball Reclaimed America.* New York: G.P. Putnam's Sons, 1999.

McFarlane, Brian. *100 Years of Hockey History.* Champaign, IL: Sagamore Pub., 1997.

Murphy, Shane M. *The Cheers and the Tears: A Healthy Alternative to the Dark Side of Youth Sports Today.* San Francisco: Jossey-Bass, 1999.

Noll, Roger G., and Andrew Zimbalist. *Sports, Jobs, and Taxes: The Economic Impact of Sports Teams and Stadiums.* Washington, D.C.: Brookings Institute, 1997.

Quirk, James P., and Rodney D. Fort. *Hard Ball: The Abuse of Power in Pro Team Sports.* Princeton: Princeton UP, 1999.

Rossi, John P. *The National Game: Baseball and American Culture.* Chicago: I. R. Dee, 2000.

Shields, David. *Black Planet: Facing Race During an NBA Season.* New York: Crown, 1999.

Silby, Caroline, Ph.D., with Shelley Smith. *Games Girls Play: Understanding and Guiding Young Female Athletes.* New York: St. Martin's P, 2000.

Smith, Lissa. *Nike Is a Goddess: The History of Women in Sports.* New York: Atlantic Monthly P, 1998.

Sperber, Murray. *Beer and Circus: How Big-Time College Sports Is Crippling Undergraduate Education.* New York: Henry Holt & Company, Inc., 2000.

Wolff, Rick. *Good Sports: The Concerned Parent's Guide to Competitive Youth Sports.* Campaign, IL: Coaches Choice, 1997.

Zimbalist, Andrew. *Unpaid Professionals: Commercialism and Conflict in Big-Time College Sports.* Princeton: Princeton UP, 1999.

# Additional Periodical Articles with Abstracts

More information on sports in America can be found in the following articles. Readers who require a more comprehensive selection are advised to consult *Reader's Guide Abstracts* and other H.W. Wilson indexes.

**American Sport.** Thomas J. McCarthy. *America* v. 182 p6 Jan. 29–Feb. 5, 2000.

McCarthy writes that professional sports have become another element of the entertainment corporate culture. With teams being purchased and sold overnight and players selling themselves to the highest bidder, he claims, fans can hardly identify with them. As Benjamin Barber contends in his book *Jihad vs. McWorld*, people are increasingly being asked to view themselves as consumers, customers, and clients rather than citizens. According to McCarthy, sports at all levels, meanwhile, are laboring under the burden of unchecked hype, greed, and attention.

**The Fumble of a Lifetime.** Paul Ruffins. *Black Issues in Higher Education* v. 17 pp34–36 April 27, 2000.

The writer explains that the propensity of athletes to get into trouble has confronted higher education institutions and sports leagues with the practical issue of creating intervention programs for their athletes. Two such intervention programs for athletes are described, and obstacles to the success of these programs are discussed.

**Professors' Group Seeks to Reform College Sports.** Erik Lords. *The Chronicle of Higher Education* v. 46 pA58 April 7, 2000.

Lords reports that the National Alliance for Collegiate Athletic Reform adopted an ambitious platform designed "to restore academic integrity, to fulfill our obligations as faculty, and to protect the welfare of all students" at a meeting in March 2000. The group's call for institutions to eliminate athletic scholarships, publicly disclose significant information about the classroom performance of sports teams, and put the faculty in charge of academic counseling for athletes is discussed.

**How the NCAA's Test-Score Rules Look from the Ground Up**. Welch Suggs. *The Chronicle of Higher Education* v. 46 ppA57–58 Oct. 8, 1999

Suggs discusses the debate over the U.S. National Collegiate Athletic Association's eligibility requirements and how they affect black students. The writer examines proposition 48, which requires the incoming freshmen to attain certain minimum SAT or ACT scores to be eligible to compete. Suggs also covers the legal battle over the proposition, along with support and criticism for it. Efforts by school administrators to prepare students and the cases of Yohance Buchanan and John Andrews are also discussed.

**Sports and Your Child: What Every Parent Should Know.** Kimberly Davis. *Ebony* v. 55 pp86–90 June 2000.

Davis explains that youth sports is one of the biggest and fastest-growing entertainment industries in America. More than 20 million American children compete in such sports as basketball, baseball, football, soccer, and gymnastics. Experts say sports teach children vital lessons about sportsmanship, discipline, respect for authority, and priority-setting. Each year, however, more than 5 million school-aged children seek emergency medical care for sports injuries, according to statistics from the U.S. Consumer Product Safety Commission. The writer provides advice for parents on how to physically and mentally prepare their children for the rigors of competition.

**The Name in the Game.** Leonard S. Greenberger. *Electric Perspectives* v. 24 pp52–61 July/Aug. 1999.

Greenberger examines how utilities are putting their names on sports facilities and other institutions in the belief that it will translate into greater profits in a newly competitive atmosphere. Competition, Greenberger explains, is affecting how energy firms like Enron Energy Services, Cinergy Corp., and Sempra Energy interact with their customers, both regionally and nationally. Positioning the utility brand is paramount for numerous firms, and a large part of brand support has nothing to do with advertising in the media. No-ad advertising, the term used to refer to sponsorships and such like, can be the solution, Greenberger asserts.

**Tarnished Gold?** Joan M. Steinauer. *Incentive* v. 173 pp18+ July 1999.

Steinauer reports on the marketing of the sponsorship of the 2002 Salt Lake Winter Games after a bribery scandal. She examines the role of Robert Prazmark, president of the Olympic Marketing and Sales for International Management Group in attracting corporate sponsors. The writer provides details on the scandal, the effect on the marketing demands of the sponsors, and information on the amount of the business of sponsoring sports events in North America.

**The Real Scandal.** Sharon Begley and Martha Brant. *Newsweek* v. 133 pp48–54 Feb. 15, 1999.

The writers assert that, despite the recent corruption controversies surrounding the International Olympic Committee, the use of dangerous, performance-enhancing drugs, or doping, is the greatest threat to international sport. They claim that doping is rampant among world-class competitors, and many athletes admit that the governing bodies of individual sports ignore the behavior of drug-takers. Begley and Brant say that drug usage may jeopardize the image, integrity, and continued existence of elite-level sport, including the Olympic Games. Sidebars list many of the performance-enhancing drugs used by some athletes and discuss some Olympians who have been caught doping.

**Up, Up and Away, Dude!** Devin Gordon. *Newsweek* v. 134 pp78–80 Jan. 1, 2000.

As Gordon reports, the world of extreme sports is becoming increasingly popular and, provided it is not taken over by corporate sponsorship, should gain even more attention in the future. He explains that sports such as baseball rely on the game itself, but extreme sports offer trick-based events that are individual and irreverent. The number of TV viewers for the X Games, extreme sport's main event, has doubled since 1994, and, Gordon speculates, it may prove more popular than the Olympics in the future.

**The Jock v. the Clock.** Claudia Kalb. *Newsweek* v. 133 pp76+ May 24, 1999.

Kalb reports that baby boomers are taking part in more aggressive sports and getting hurt more frequently because they are unfit or place too many demands on their bodies. She says these "weekend warriors" tear ligaments, cartilage, and tendons, which are especially vulnerable to wear and injury, sending millions to orthopedists annually. In people 40 and over, Kalb says, injuries are more often chronic conditions from years of overuse, routine aging, or flare-ups of past injuries. The writer discusses several common perils of middle age, describes a number of new treatments, and offers advice on avoiding injury.

**March Madness.** Laurie Sandell. *New York* v. 33 pp13–14 April 3, 2000.

Sandell focuses on the National Collegiate Athletic Association (NCAA) betting pools at Wall Street's trading floors during the playoffs in the month of March. She explains the typical betting arrangement and relates stories about the losses of some Wall Street traders. Sandell also provides details on the bidding activities of the traders for the NCAA basketball teams.

**The Minority Quarterback.** Ira Berkow. *New York Times* p1 July 2, 2000.

Berkow focuses on the controversy surrounding the selection of a white quarterback for predominantly African-American Southern University's football team. He examines the experiences of the quarterback, Marcus Jacoby, at the school and the resentment of Jacoby's teammates. Berkow also provides examples of racism against blacks elsewhere in Louisiana's higher education system. He then details the football team's record with Jacoby as quarterback and factors affecting Jacoby's decision to quit the team and the school.

**Baseball Must Come Clean on Its Darkest Secret.** Steve Kettmann. *New York Times* sec. 8 p13 Aug. 20, 2000.

The writer criticizes the use of steroids by baseball players. He reviews the history of the drug androstenedione and criticizes the reluctance of Major League Baseball to take action on the drug. He also gives his views on steroid use.

**Samaranch: Olympic Savior or Spoiler?** Jere Longman. *New York Times* sec. 8 p1 Sept. 10, 2000.

Longman focuses on Juan Antonio Samaranch, president of the International Olympic Committee. The writer examines how he handled problems which faced the Olympics when he began in 1980 and how decisions he made have contributed to corruption, the use of drugs, and the size of the Olympics. Longman includes an example of favors Samaranch granted to Jean-Claude Ganga of the Republic of Congo.

**Women Move Closer to Olympic Equality.** Jere Longman. *New York Times* sec.1 p1 Aug. 20, 2000.

Longman discusses the presence of female athletes at the 2000 Olympic Games in Sydney, Australia. The writer examines the number of women competing and events that are traditionally male-only that have been added for women, including weight lifting. Longman explains that interest in women's sports has been increasing and provides brief profiles of several females who will compete in Sydney, including pole vaulter Stacy Dragila and triathlete Jennifer Gutierez.

**What a Racket.** Andre L. Christopher. *Parks & Recreation* v. 34 pp54–61 Oct. 1999.

Christopher discusses the USA Tennis Plan for Growth initiative to promote and develop the growth of tennis in the United States. He examines the percentage of Americans who go to parks and recreation departments to play tennis, as well as factors for the success of community tennis programs and the penetration of tennis into the adult market.

**Olympicgate: Why It Happened.** John Fry. *Ski* v. 63 pp21+ March/April 1999.

Fry asserts that the Olympic movement became corrupt long before the explosion of the votes-for-sale scandal involving the Salt Lake Organizing Committee. He explores what the Olympics symbolized during the earlier part of the 20th century and the decline of amateurism. Fry also gives an account of Olympic sports marketing.

**Hey, Fans: Sit on It!** E. M. Swift. *Sports Illustrated* v. 92 pp70+ May 15, 2000.

Swift focuses on the high cost of attending major league sporting events, particularly the increase in ticket prices for National Football League, National Hockey League, National Basketball Association, and Major League Baseball games. As Swift reports, reasons for the inflation range from player salaries to frequent patronage from corporate customers willing to pay high prices. The result, the writer explains, has been a decline in ticket demand, including the decision of many fans not to purchase season tickets. Swift also discusses the competition of other recreational activities in southern Florida and the effect of television on fans' decisions not to attend games.

**Ad In.** Kevin O'Keefe. *Tennis* v. 36 pp10–12 March 2000.

O'Keefe writes that tennis has suddenly become popular among advertisers. In the eyes of agencies and their clients, he says, tennis is a cool activity that will sell mainstream goods and services, including hotel suites, health products, beer, investments, and watches. Once depicted by the media as an elitist sport, tennis is now viewed by the advertising business as a "good fit" for enhancing brand image. A number of tennis-themed advertisements are discussed.

**The Ongoing Controversy over Title IX.** George J. Bryjak. *USA Today* v. 129 pp62–63 July 2000.

Bryjak explains the opposition to Title IX, part of the Educational Amendments Act of 1972, which asserts that all schools in receipt of federal funding must provide equal opportunity for males and females. Sports economist Andrew Zimbalist claims the National Collegiate Athletic Association and President Ronald Reagan made several attempts to derail the law, as have various politicians recently. According to Bryjak, opponents say the provision's quota system is unfair because it forces significant numbers of men's teams to be reduced or eliminated as a way of counteracting the cost of women's sports programs.

**Parents Are Dying to Win.** Mary Lord *U.S. News & World Report* v. 129 p28 July 24, 2000.

According to Lord, big-league violence has exploded over children's sports. Enraged parents have fired guns at pee-wee football games, offered to bribe young pitchers to bean opposing batters, and rioted on sports fields. To protect themselves against such violence, Lord explains, communities are increasingly going on the offense, with over 170 city and suburban sports associations instituting programs in parental conduct. The opinions of psychologists on sports violence are examined.

**Objects of the Game.** Joanna Cagan. *Village Voice* v. 45 p182 Aug. 30–Sept. 5, 2000.

Cagan presents information on the increasing number of female athletes posing nude for several publications, along with public reaction to the trends. She also addresses the implications of the willingness of athletes to pose and factors responsible for turning women athletes into sex symbols.

**An Athletic Arms Race.** Jeff D. Opdyke. *Wall Street Journal* pB1 Aug. 23, 2000.

Opdyke reports on the efforts that universities are making to draw more fans and attract the best athletes by adding more seats and facilities to their athletic stadiums. He discusses the number of schools that have completed or are in the midst of projects and the amount of money they are spending on the projects. He also examines how Louisiana State University best illustrates the trends driving the stadium-expansion craze.

# Index